BINDING AND REPAIRING BOOKS BY HAND

Binding and Repairing Books by Hand

David Muir

With drawings by Richard Bawden

B.T. BATSFORD LTD, LONDON

First published 1978
Copyright David Muir 1978

Filmset on 12 on 14pt 'Monophoto' Photina by
Servis Filmsetting Ltd, Manchester

Printed in Great Britain by The Anchor Press Ltd, Tiptree, Essex
for the publishers, B.T. Batsford Ltd,
4 Fitzhardinge Street, London W1H 0AH

ISBN 0 7134 0677 1

Contents

List of illustrations   6

Introduction   9

1 Tools for repairing, basic materials   11

2 Repairing heads and tails, corners and torn pages   17

3 Preliminary steps to rebacking   29

4 Rebacking in cloth and leather   48

5 Disbinding, resewing, trimming edges   57

6 Rebinding a cloth book   77

7 Rebinding quarter and half leather books   93

8 Rebinding full leather books   106

9 Gold finishing   111

   Glossary   115

   List of materials and suppliers   118

   Index   120

List of illustrations

1 Parts of a bound book   *page 8*
2 Basic tools   *10*
3 Sharpening the paring knife on a whet stone   *12*
4 Sharpening paring knife on wood   *13*
5 Lifting a cloth side   *16*
6 Head or tail piece   *18*
7 Inserting head or tail piece   *19*
8 Turning in head or tail piece   *20*
9 Repaired head   *20*
10 Paring leather   *22*
11 Making a head cap   *23*
12 Corner repair   *25*
13 Repair of torn page   *26*
14 Pasting endpaper   *31*
15 Gluepot   *32*
16 Lying press   *33*
17 Spine ready for mull in holding press   *35*
18 Gluing on Phillip's hollow in holding press   *36*
19 Three fold hollow: cutting   *37*
20 Three fold hollow: gluing first flap   *38*
21 Three fold hollow: gluing second flap   *39*
22 Three fold hollow: trimming excess   *40*
23 Cutting edge of three fold hollow   *41*
24 Marking for raised bands   *43*
25 Measuring string for raised bands   *44*
26 Placing raised bands   *45*
27 Raised bands in position   *45*
28 Threading silk for headband   *46*
29 Winding silk for headband   *47*
30 Pasting cloth for reback   *49*
31 Attaching new cloth to spine   *49*
32 Turn in cloth reback   *50*
33 Firming end of cloth case   *50*
34 Fitting new leather to spine   *55*
35 Tightening leather turn in   *55*
36 Small nipping press   *59*
37 Large nipping press   *60*
38 Sawing a book for sewing   *62*
39 The sewing press   *63*
40 A made-up sewing press   *64*
41 Attaching sewing cords to key   *65*
42 Starting to sew a book   *66*
43 Making a kettle stitch   *67*

44 Figure-of-8 sewing onto raised cords   *69*
45 Tapping up book before pressing   *72*
46 Fluffing the sewing cords   *73*
47 Board cutter   *75*
48 Using a plough   *76*
49 Backing and cutting boards   *78*
50 Putting backing boards to the book   *79*
51 Hammering the sections   *80*
52 Tapping down final edge   *81*
53 The rounding of the book   *82*
54 Cutting a side board   *83*
55 Folding back strip   *84*
56 Cutting a hollow for spine   *84*
57 Sticking down sewing cords   *85*
58 Cutting out cloth for cover   *87*
59 Gluing cloth for cover   *88*
60 Putting book on new cover   *89*
61 Turning in cloth edges   *90*
62 Bending in corner overlap   *90*
63 Pasting down endpaper   *91*
64 Preparing to lace in a board   *95*
65 Lacing in a board   *95*
66 Hammering laced in cords smooth   *96*
67 Notching corner of board   *101*
68 Turning in a leather corner
69 Marking leather spine for trimming   *101*
70 Trimming leather inside book   *103*
71 Pasting down endpaper of half-leather binding   *104*
72 Drying pasted, leather-bound book   *104*
73 Turning in full leather corner   *108*
74 Feathering leather corner   *109*
75 Polishing iron   *110*
76 Using a polishing iron   *110*
77 Some tools for gold lettering   *111*
78 The finishing press and gold cushion   *112*
79 Cutting gold leaf   *113*

1 Parts of a bound book

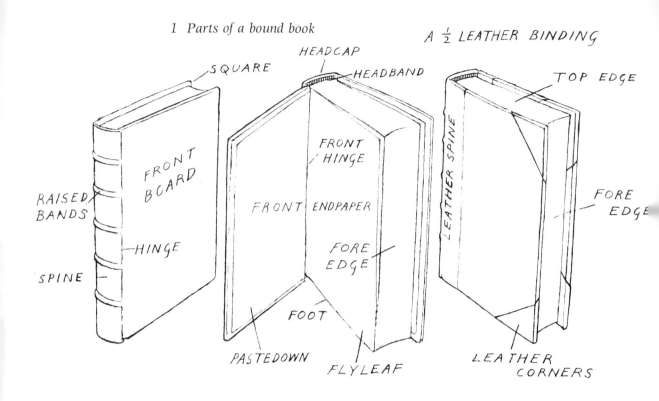

A ½ LEATHER BINDING

SQUARE

HEADCAP

HEADBAND

FRONT BOARD

RAISED BANDS

HINGE

SPINE

FRONT HINGE

FRONT ENDPAPER

FORE EDGE

FOOT

PASTEDOWN

FLYLEAF

LEATHER SPINE

TOP EDGE

FORE EDGE

LEATHER CORNERS

Introduction

In the following chapters I will be attempting to explain some of the intricacies and problems of book-binding and repairing. I should say, right away, that these skills are not acquired in five minutes. All I can hope to do is to show the way I tackle the jobs I have to do all the time. The apprentice-ship for book-binding is six years for forwarding, likewise for gold finishing and this, remember, is keeping at it all the time during a working week.

I find I am always learning, even after many years of constant practice, so please do not expect perfection quickly. You must be prepared to persevere even if you are disappointed with your early efforts. Although it takes time to acquire great skill, it is possible to achieve respectable results given enthusiasm, patience and, above all practice, and these results can be achieved reasonably quickly.

You *must* accept that it is necessary to do each job a few times before success is achieved. Unless you are naturally very gifted most of your early attempts at new jobs will make you cross, sad, or both; this happens to most beginners at all crafts. I have difficulty remembering my own problems when I started book-binding, but I can easily remember my frustration when recently I began trying to master the game of golf. However, with dogged persistence and fanatical practice I soon achieved great pleasure from this skill.

So you will need all the enthusiasm you can muster to learn about the repairing of books, because even to the professional there are times when a job seems hopeless. Yet when it is finished you think back and wonder why you made such a fuss at the time.

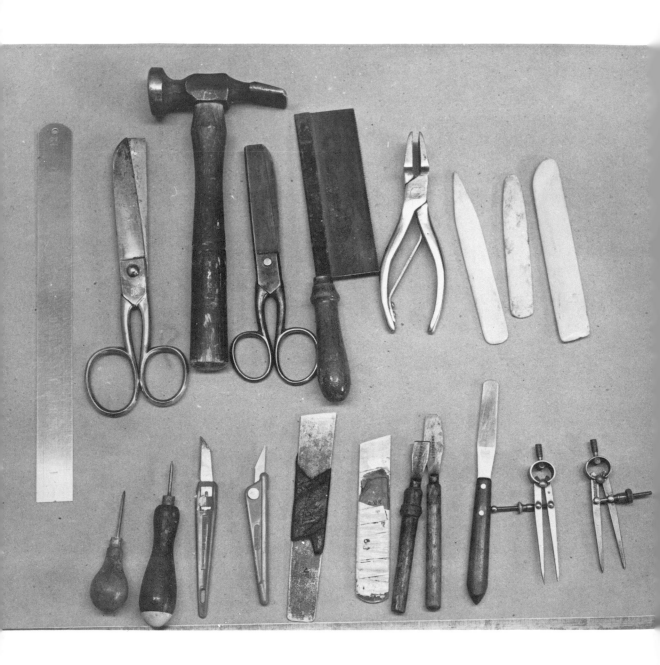

2 Basic tools: top, left to right, metal foot rule, large shears, backing hammer, smaller shears, tenon saw, band nippers, three bone folders; bottom, left to right, two bradawls, two cutting knives, two paring knives, three palette lifting knives, two pairs of dividers

1 Tools for repairing, basic materials

It is surprising what may be accomplished with a few simple hand tools. These items may become treasured friends; I would rate one or two of my own tools as such, having had them since I was first apprenticed. You must have at least one each of the following: bone folder 5″, one pair large shears, one pair medium sized scissors (for delicate work), 12″ rule (metal), one knife, one paring knife, a few mixed sized brushes for applying paste etc., one palette knife 4″ (obtainable from any art shop), two whet stones (fine and rough), 3-in-one oil.

You will generally be able to complete most repair jobs with the above tools. However, if you wish to tackle such work as rebinding, etc., then the following tools are needed: one backing hammer, one tenon saw, one 24″ rule (metal), one large folder 8–10″, one pair band nippers, one awl, pair dividers. There are also a number of additional larger items for the enthusiast, but these are not hand tools and will be described and shown in later chapters.

It is unfortunate that the above list of tools must be purchased in most cases, as they are not items which one may make. The exception to this is the paring knife. This particular tool is the one the skilled man will be using a hundred times a day. In fact, many craftsmen have two or three of these knives and they use each one for a specific job, e.g. one for paring or thinning leather, and one for lifting and cutting leather. The knife for paring must be kept sharp enough to shave a man's beard and therefore would suffer if used for cutting and lifting. You may make a paring knife from any suitable piece of strong flat metal. I have seen very good knives made from old metal saw blades; the large saws that is, not the thin small ones. A good place to find one of the latter is a garage, which will also be sure to have an electric emery wheel which you may use to shape the blade and remove the teeth. After the handle has been wound with some tape you may begin the process of sharpening the knife to a good edge. This is done with the whet stones. If you put some oil on the rough stone you will find that when the knife is moved up and down the surface a kind of oily paste is formed. This grinds the metal down until the edge you need is attained. Try to achieve the look of a hollow ground knife such as you would see in a shop (fig. 3). You will not achieve this, but

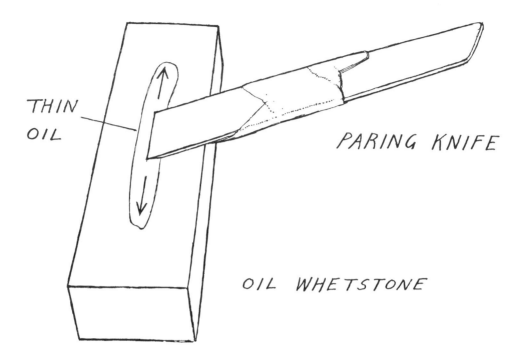

THIN OIL

PARING KNIFE

OIL WHETSTONE

trying to do so will give you the correct edge. The back of the knife is never sharpened and must remain very flat. If you find you have achieved a burr you should place the knife flat on the stone, sharp side up, and move it back and forth two or three times. On reaching a reasonable state of sharpness, complete this stage by using the fine whet stone. Once the work with the stones is done, honing on a wooden surface is very good for additional sharpness. All that is needed is a plank of wood 16″ long by 4″ wide which should be smooth. The plank must be fixed to a bench at waist height and the knife moved back and forth over the plank with as much downward force as possible (fig. 4). This action is a slowish rhythmical honing and is done first one way then the other to remove burrs from the knife. You will find this honing will keep the blade sharp for some time if you do it regularly when using the knife. When it no longer makes the knife sharp you must return to the whet stones.

To continue with items you will require, we now come to

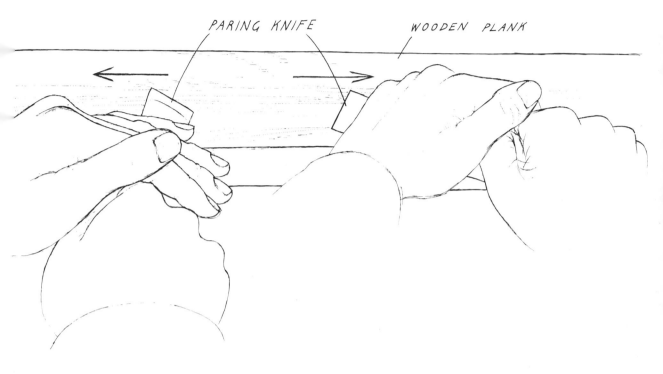

4 *Sharpening paring knife on wood*

PARING KNIFE

WOODEN PLANK

materials. As we are concerned mainly with repairing at the moment I shall tell you only the materials for that. The main item you need is fortunately cheap: cold water paste powder. This is to be found in all D.I.Y. shops and is used for hanging wallpaper. One word of warning, however – do not use cellulose-based pastes but stick to cold water flour paste or water-based pastes. I say this because you can always wash off the latter when it has spread where you did not want it to go and it is also ideal for use with leather.

You will need furbishing cream for leather books (see List of Suppliers). Finally there are the materials, leather and cloth. It is possible to get pieces of cloth from old unwanted books by taking the cloth from the old boards and cutting it into usable pieces. Leather, however, is a problem. Firstly it is expensive and secondly it comes in largish skins which are not usually sold except in the complete skin. If you attend a technical college you should be able to acquire some pieces there, also cloth, but if not the only thing is to buy some from one of the suppliers, as listed. If your repairs are mainly to calf- or sheep-bound books you should have a skin of aniline sheep which is sold by Hewit and Sons. This is excellent leather for repairing and may also be used for rebinding. One of its main attributes is that it stains beautifully. Books are, of course, different colours and it is necessary to match the colours when repairing so as to achieve an invisible repair. Sheep is the cheapest of the four types of leather. The average skin is about 8–9 square feet. The other kinds of leather are calf, goat (niger and morocco) and cowhide. These leathers are expensive and are mainly used for rebinding purposes. However, to reback a morocco book you should use the appropriate leather and for hefty tomes such as folios a strong cowhide is useful. You will of course require the stains to colour the leather and these may be obtained from shoe shops or general stores. The stain you require is an ordinary shoe leather dye, not a suede dye or cleaner. *Radium* and *Meltonian* are two I have used. The stain is not often used neat; you must buy methylated spirits and weaken the solution into softer colours, e.g. grey instead of harsh black, and also mix the colours to give black-brown, a very useful colour. There are endless combinations and only personal experimentation will give you the colour you require.

To apply the stain you should use a pad of cotton wool which will spread the stain evenly and without streaks. When you have finished a piece of leather-staining do not throw away the cotton wool as it will retain the stain and may be used again by just wetting with meths. Another useful item when staining is a pair of rubber gloves which prevent one's fingers becoming all sorts of garish colours.

A lot cheaper than stain is permanganate of potash, obtainable from any chemist. A small amount mixed with water will stain leather a rich brown. You should be most careful when staining leather to use very dilute amounts of stain, unless the end colour required is very dark. The main problem with using bottled leather dyes of the *Radium* type is that once spread on the leather they may not be removed and therefore it is best where possible to use permanganate of potash. If you need a colour other than brown and must use a *Radium*-type stain then put a little on and partly dry it; then, if it doesn't match, add a further coat and so on until you have the perfect match. After a little practice you will find it is possible to get the matching colour with one or two coats of stain. Some books have patterns of darker stain which have been put on over a lighter colour and perhaps the most common of these is 'spotting'. Spotting is done by dipping a nail brush into the stain and then flicking a knife across the bristles to give a spray of spots. The more stain on the brush the larger the spots. (It is most advisable to practice on a piece of newspaper before spotting direct onto some leather.) You will find that your stain is very useful for touching up leather and cloth books whose binding has lost its colour through wear and tear. After applying the right colour a little paste is spread on the rubbed part. When this is quite dry the furbishing cream is applied, in the case of a leather book, and the book may, after polishing, look as good as new.

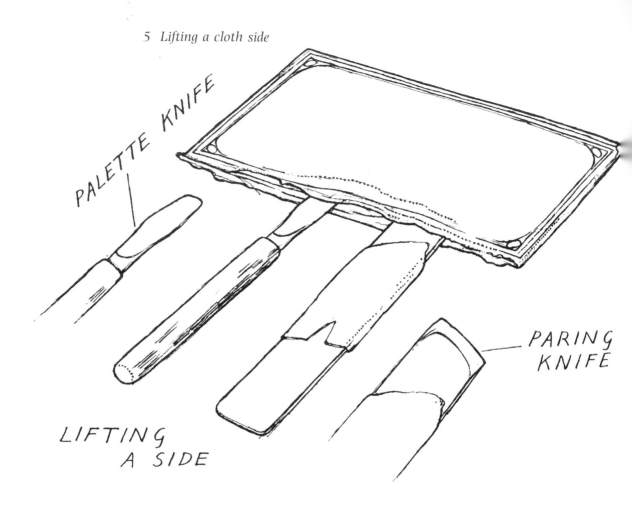

PALETTE KNIFE

PARING
KNIFE

LIFTING
A SIDE

2 Repairing heads and tails, corners and torn pages

Having acquired the materials you need for simple repair work and achieved the right colour of the damaged volume you may proceed with the actual repair of a book.

Heads and Tails

The most common and necessary repair is to the heads and tails of books, be they cloth or leather. Firstly we shall repair the head, or top, of a cloth book. It might be as well at this time to explain that the heads of books are often damaged by careless taking down from a shelf. Sometimes books are crammed onto a shelf so tightly packed that when someone tries to remove a volume he attempts to prise it loose by pulling it out from the top. The result is that the back of the book starts to tear at the top and sides and often is completely torn off and lost. So – please – do take care when taking a book from the shelf, and if you see someone else commit the crime show them the error of their ways!

CLOTH   Figure 9 below shows where you should start your repair, namely, with a cut along the inside of each board. Please note that as the cut is made, with the paring knife, the open board of the book should be resting on a suitable sized block or another book. This is most important as otherwise you may further damage the joints of the book. Having made a cut of an inch or two the inside cloth and endpaper should be carefully lifted. This job will be performed much more easily if you use the palette knife to give you a start as its thin blade slips easily under the cloth you are lifting. After the initial lifting has been successful you may like to use a broader knife and just lever up the material you wish to lift. I suggest this because the blade of the palette knife is very narrow and too much pressure may be brought to bear on a small area; by using the paring knife you will lift most of the inside in one operation. Your attention must now be turned to the outside, which is lifted in the same way as the inside but will differ slightly due to the back or spine of the book, which should have a thin piece of card attached to the cloth. Your repair should go between the card and cloth, so gently separate them. You are now ready for your new piece of cloth which you have already chosen for its

SHAPE OF PIECE OF CLOTH

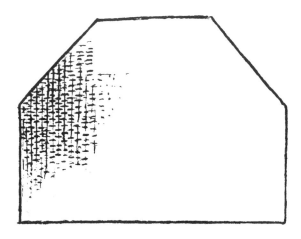

FOR REPAIRING A HEAD OR TAIL

matching colour. You will need a square piece of cloth which is large enough to cover the torn parts of the book and also enough to turn into the inside. Your finished piece should look like that in figure 6, and you may like to try it for size before using any sticking agent. You do need to have an almost perfect fit as if it is too big you will have an embarrassment of cloth, and if too small it will not cover all the tears. So try out your piece and trim to match.

Now you are ready to use your sticking agent, and at this time I would recommend that you use the paste powder I have mentioned before. There are other adhesives such as P.V.A. (see glossary) glue which may be used, but I must stress that paste is safe because the beginner will spread quite a bit of the stuff in all the wrong places as well as the right ones and paste may be easily washed off with ordinary water and cotton wool. You should mix your paste carefully, and not too much at a time; a little goes a long way. Just add a small amount of paste to water in a saucer until you have a thick porridge type of paste, which will be ready for use immediately. You will need to paste both sides of the piece of cloth you are using for repair and also the cloth and board of the book. The only place which must remain free of paste is the inside of the back with the strip of thin card previously mentioned. You need this to remain dry as it is known as the hollow, enabling the back of the cover to spring away from the book when you open it to read. Having pasted all the right places you stand the book on its tail and open it from the middle as shown; you will then find it much easier to insert the piece of cloth (see figures 7 and 8). Using the palette knife, push the cloth right into the places too small for your fingers to go. Having got the new cloth in the right place you may stick down all the old cloth and then turn the book onto its back to finish the job. All you have to do now is to turn the

7 Inserting head or tail piece

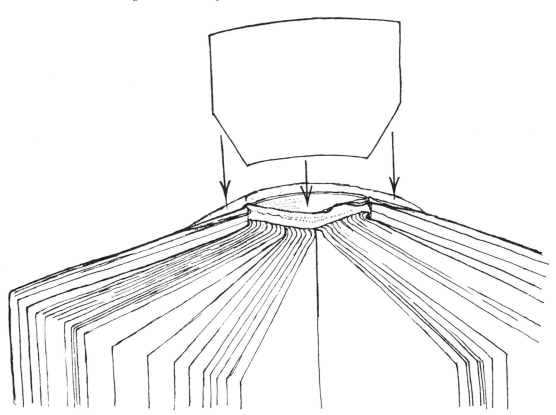

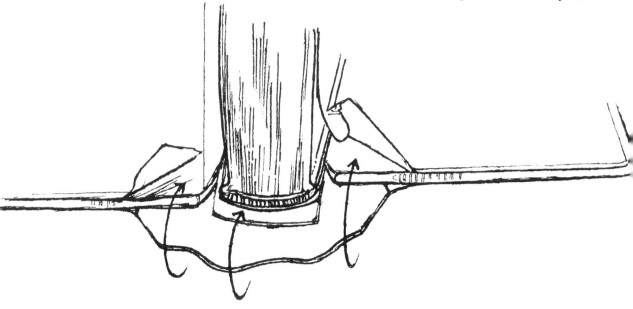

8 *Turning in head or tail piece*

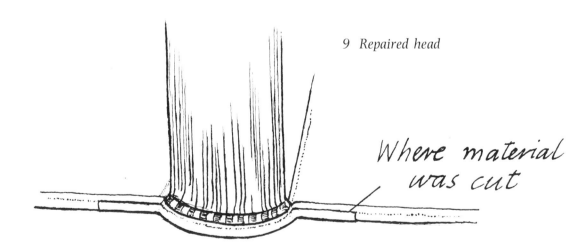

9 *Repaired head*

Where material
was cut

The head of a book that has
been repaired

cloth in and under the endpapers, pasting down the endpapers behind, giving a neat and strong repair. If you have done the job neatly and matched the colour of cloth well, very little of the repair will be seen (fig. 9).

It is important to note that the repair I have described, and the one I am about to, are just that, repairs. If the joint along the spine of the book is broken along its entire length or nearly so, then you should reback the book, a job I will describe in the next chapter. In other words these jobs are for the person with a few tools and materials who would like to improve the state of those books that he or she can, e.g. cloth books not too badly damaged.

LEATHER The other repair of this type is that of the leather book which although of a different material requires a very similar job. In some ways the repair is easier, as leather is a very supple material when wet and pasty. There is one snag to this job: the paring or thinning of the leather. I am afraid this particular stage of the repair must either be learnt by trial and error or, much better, demonstrated by an expert. You will not learn to pare leather quickly; it will take a great many hours of practice and you are bound to tear and damage many pieces of leather before you make much progress, but persistence will bring a reward that will give you much pleasure when you have reached a reasonable standard. You will find paring a little easier if you have the right surface to work on, i.e. a smooth piece of marble or litho-stone, as in figure 10. Your piece of leather should be thin enough to fold twice and stay flat and should also be of an even thickness and not all bumps and ridges. You will understand the meaning of the last sentence when you are learning to pare, as this is one of the most difficult skills to master. Now, assuming you have your piece of leather stained and pared and you have lifted the leather and endpapers of the book, you may find that, unlike in cloth books, the back or spine of the leather volume does not always lift away from the book when it is opened. This is what is known, not surprisingly, as a tight back and was the only method of binding books in the eighteenth century, and earlier. Now we use the hollow spine and you will find that most leather books have this. If you have a tight-back book to repair you will

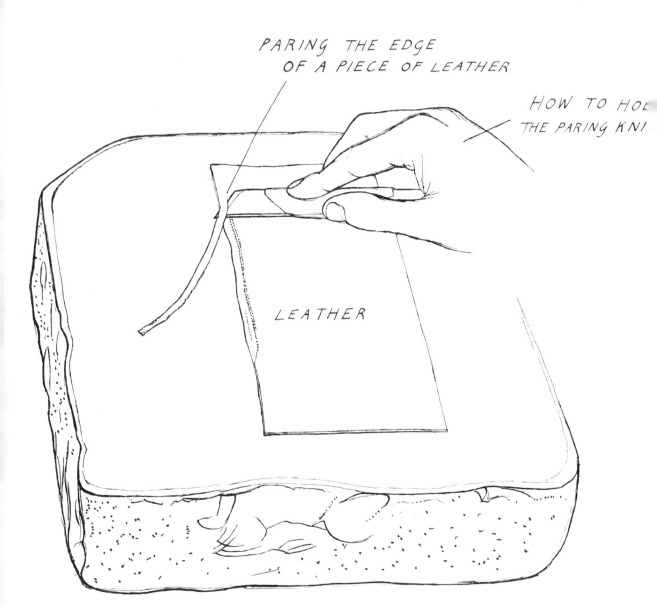

PARING THE EDGE
OF A PIECE OF LEATHER

HOW TO HOL
THE PARING KNI

LEATHER

LITHO
STONE

find the spine very difficult to lift. If this is so you should not worry but just stick the new leather over the top. In most cases, however, with care you should be able to lift enough to complete head or tail repairs. This then will proceed exactly as for a cloth job, leaving the spine hollow where it was hollow and tight where tight. Again, carefully stick down all the old leather over the new and wash with wet cotton wool. One difference between the cloth repair and the leather one is the headcap in the leather repair. A headcap is the piece of leather on the very top and bottom of the spine and covers the headband. You should have enough leather left from your repair to complete this small job. If you find that you do not have enough leather to cover the headband you must pull a little more out, doing this while the book is closed, using the fingertips or nails. A piece of strong button thread should be used to pull the leather tight into the notches in the boards next to the headbands (fig. 11). It will then be possible to shape and flatten the headcap

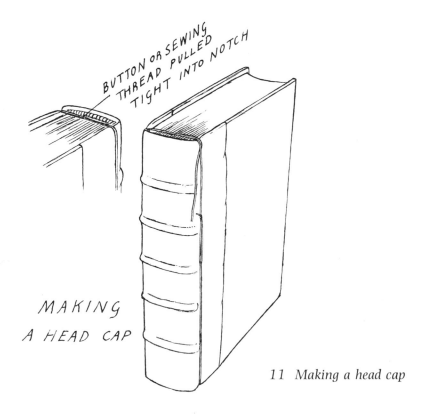

11 Making a head cap

with the bone folder. Afterwards leave the book closed up to dry. One other small point is that it is wise to leave small strips of greaseproof paper inside to protect the endpapers from paste and damp. The type of paper you need is the same as you would find in a cornflake packet; in fact this is what I use myself, and it costs nothing.

Corners

As well as heads and tails of books, corners suffer a great deal. The corners of cloth books are usually reasonably repaired by being tapped gently and then pasted and left to dry, as are some leather book corners. However, some leather corners crumble and begin to put the pages in danger. When this has happened to one or more corners, action should be taken before the content of the book itself suffers. Firstly, you should cut the leather along the inside of the board just as when repairing a head or tail. Again the leather should be lifted carefully and also the inside leather and endpapers. This will expose the damaged board which should then be carefully split. You will need some thin card which should be cut into a triangle and inserted within the cut. This will provide the basis for a new 90° corner which of course was the shape of the original. When you insert the piece of card you will need to paste it on both sides and then clamp it into the cut with some suitable tool such as a large bulldog clip. When this has had several hours to dry you may build up the corner to its original size, using anything you may find suitable. I have found that small chippings from leather parings mixed with paste make a very suitable fill-in and when dry form a smooth and solid repair (fig. 12).

You will now be ready to repair the leather. On many corners the leather repair is all that is needed to bring the corner back to strength. You will need a piece of leather stained and pared that will be just big enough to repair the missing leather and also make good the edges of the board. I must stress that the leather should be reasonably thin, otherwise an ugly bulky repair will result. You must realise that in places double the thickness of leather will be present and this will be impossible to conceal if the leather is left very thick.

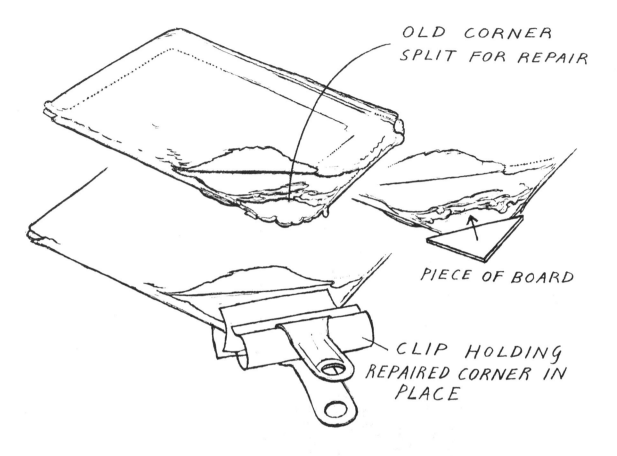

OLD CORNER
SPLIT FOR REPAIR

PIECE OF BOARD

CLIP HOLDING
REPAIRED CORNER IN
PLACE

This applies to most repair and rebacking jobs. Although it is a lot to ask of a beginner, one should always strive for perfection which will come if care and persistence are present. Having pasted the new piece of leather and the surface to receive it you should apply it to the corner and turn it in. Leather is very pleasant to use when wet and the corner should join together on the inside very easily and compactly. When the new leather has dried you may paste down the old leather on top, trying as much as possible to cover the new leather, using the paste to heal the cuts you made, but wiping over with damp cotton wool when finished, then leaving to dry with the repaired corners standing away from the pages so that the dampness will not affect them.

Tears

Repair of a torn page is one of the easier jobs and may be completed with the minimum of materials. All you need is a small amount of paste and some very thin tissue paper that print may be seen through. Check your tissue before using it by placing a piece over a printed page and if it is of the correct quality you will be able to read the words easily. There are some tissues that are rather opaque and therefore not suitable. (Japanese lens tissue is the best.)

To commence the repair, you should place a piece of waste paper underneath the tear to catch any spare paste that may come through. Then you spread a little paste all along the tear, making sure that the area covered by the paste does not exceed $\frac{1}{8}''$ either side of the tear. A small brush is the obvious thing for this work. It is a great help to have the paste the right thickness so that it spreads evenly – use just enough to stick the piece of tissue which you will place over the top of the tear. You should have a generous piece of tissue so that after the paste has dried you are able to tear

13 *Repair of torn page*

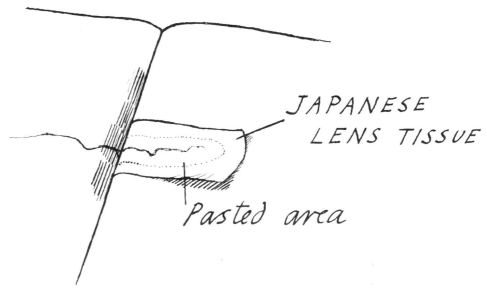

JAPANESE
LENS TISSUE

Pasted area

Repairing a tear in a page

off the unstuck part leaving the tear mended by a thin strip of pasted tissue (fig. 13). If the tear is very long or the paper heavy it may be necessary to repair both sides of the page, but for smallish tears one side will do.

You will also be able to use your paste for sticking down any loose pieces of leather or cloth, especially lettering labels which may be coming loose or right off. Corners too may last some time longer if pasted up.

Furbishing

When leather volumes have been repaired or pasted they tend to become unnaturally dry due to the action of paste and water. On completion of all the repairs and after a suitable period to allow for complete dryness, the leather volumes should be furbished. Only one person in a thousand ever seems to furbish their leather books, which seems unfortunate as this job does not take very long and will preserve the life of a leather binding for many years if done once a year. Leather needs to be kept supple which is what the furbishing cream helps to do, at the same time forming a sort of protective skin on the surface to keep out damp and other harmful substances present in the atmosphere. Tobacco and open-fire smoke are very harmful to books in general and these two pollutants should be outlawed from any library. I realise that many people like to have open coal or wood log fires in winter, and people do smoke. But these activities *are* harmful to books and should you wish to keep your collection in the best possible state it should be in a room where smoke or smoking is never allowed. While we are on the subject, temperature is also important – a steady 60–65°F being the ideal temperature.

Now back to the furbishing, which is no more or less than rubbing the cream into the leather with a soft cloth, making sure to include the edges of the boards and headcaps of the spine, leaving to dry for an hour or two and then polishing up with another dry soft cloth. Many people use the British Museum formula, which although very good is inclined to be a trifle sticky. The one that I have found most satisfactory is *Pliancreme*. Details are given in the list at the back of this book.

The above words on furbishing are probably the most important in this book as many bindings could be saved and much work avoided if only people would do this small chore regularly.

3 Preliminary steps to rebacking

We now arrive at more difficult repairs. First, rebacking, which entails the renewing of a complete spine, although quite often it is possible to replace the old back on top of the new one. This would be particularly desirable with a large set of books where just one volume needs rebacking. Unfortunately the problem of the tight back makes life very difficult here, as on many occasions it is not possible to lift the old back, and therefore it must be sacrificed if the repair is to be done.

Cleaning spine and lifting sides

Firstly, then, we shall prepare a cloth book for rebacking and secondly a leather volume.

CLOTH   If you still have the old back of a cloth volume and you wish to replace it, then put it on one side: this also applies to the back that is barely attached to the boards. You may find that the spine under the old back is covered with a paper or thin card which is loose. This should be carefully scraped off until you come to a canvas-like material with quite a large weave, which enables the glue on the spine to come right through the holes and trap the mesh into forming a union with the book. This is called the mull. The paper is put on afterwards as a finish and also for strength. If the mull or glue should be cracked and flaking you may have to remove that also, but quite often they remain hard and firm. Having cleaned the spine properly you may turn your attention to lifting the sides. Please do not be tempted to lift the sides before cleaning the spine, because you do not want bits of paper and glue to get under the lifted flaps of the old cloth.

The first stage of lifting will be exactly as for head and tail repairs; namely, always lift the inside first, followed by the outside. Again the palette knife is useful here, especially to give you a start. Once you have the edge of the cloth lifted you may find the larger paring knife better, using it as a sort of lever (see fig. 5) and cutting where necessary. The broader width of the paring knife does not put so much pressure on a small area and therefore does not stretch the old material quite as much as the palette knife would, but the paring knife is a difficult tool with which to begin a lifting job, so I would recommend making just the smallest start, even $\frac{1}{4}''$, with the palette knife.

You need to lift the old sides back to at least 2", being as careful as possible that no holes or tears are made in the cloth, and that only the cloth is lifted, not the board underneath. The final look of your work depends very much on this part of the reback, so you should take extra care in the process.

LEATHER   To lift a leather side is the same operation as for a cloth book, but is often much harder owing to the fragile nature of some old leather books. I have seen examples where the whole operation has been missed out and the new leather put on top of the old. This is not only cheating, but can also look very ugly; people who tend to do this sort of reback usually do not match the colours of their repairs and the whole job looks messy.

Before lifting your leather sides you will find that the preparation of the spine slightly differs from that for a cloth book. The leather books with hollow backs are obvious as soon as you open the book, and again you may wish to save and replace either the whole back, or just the label, if there is one. The tight back variety may have a smooth spine or raised bands. If the spine is smooth and you do not wish to save the old back, you may scrape away all the old leather until the spine is clean and firm. If, however, there are raised bands on a tight back book, these are part of the sewing of the book and may not be removed, unless you need to re-sew.

The approach here is to scrape carefully away the leather on the panels between the bands, taking great care not to damage them, or the sewing thread, which can often be seen passing over the bands and back into the book.

Now that you have the method of lifting the leather and cloth books the next stage is to prepare for using the new materials. In the case of the tight back book with bands the leather will have to go on to the back, just as the original did, so we may leave that job until we are ready to put on the leather.

Mull for new endpapers
The cloth book, with its mull and boards still firmly attached, will
also be quite ready for its reback, but if the mull has broken at the
joints, or is coming away from the spine, you will have to make
some adjustments before the actual rebacking. This depends to a
great extent on whether the endpapers are to be preserved or not.
If new endpapers are to be inserted (fig. 14) then a new piece of
mull may be glued to the back of the book and then folded under
the boards (see rebinding in cloth, chapter 6).

14 *Pasting endpaper*

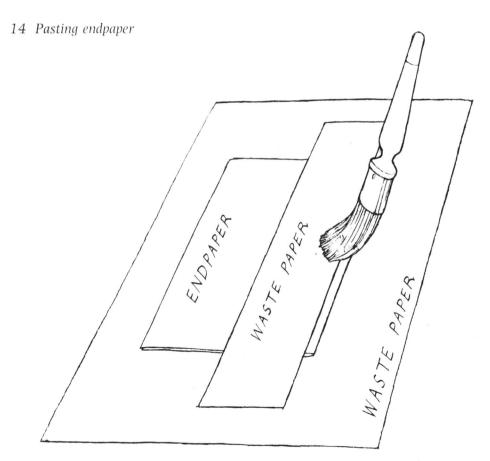

PASTING A DOUBLE SHEET OR ENDPAPER
OR ATTACHING TO FRONT OR BACK OF BOOK

For gluing you must have a glue pot (fig. 15) which comprises one pot inside another. The outside pot holds water, which is heated; the inside pot holds the crystals which,iwhen added to hot water form a brown, very sticky glue. The water in the outside pot is kept continuously simmering so as to keep the glue nice and runny.

You must have a special brush for the glue and this is left continuously in the pot, even when it is not in use. When using

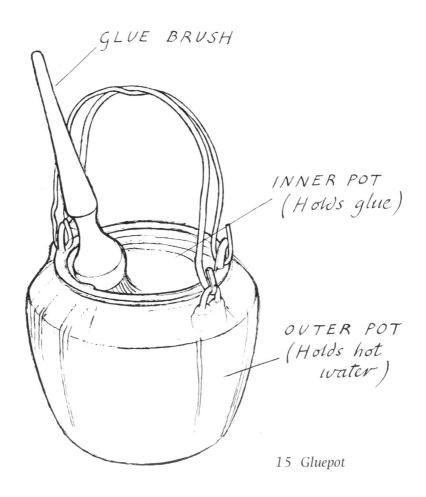

GLUE BRUSH

INNER POT
(Holds glue)

OUTER POT
(Holds hot
water)

15 Gluepot

glue on the back of a book you need what is known as a lying press (fig. 16); although for our present purpose a smaller finishing press would do. The lying press has several uses which will become apparent when we come to rebinding a book.

You should place the book in the press (fig. 17) with the boards slightly away from the spine, so as not to get the glue on them. Make sure you have all the tools you need at hand because once you begin using the glue everything must go smoothly before it should dry.

16 *Lying press*

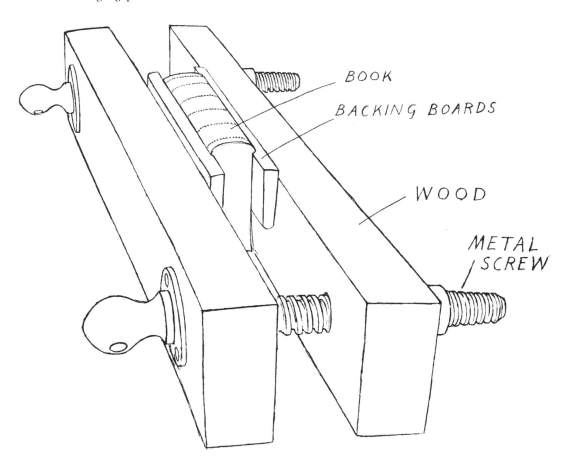

BOOK

BACKING BOARDS

WOOD

METAL
SCREW

You should have a folder, shears, your piece of mull cut to the right size, and some thickish wrapping paper – which will be stuck on top of the mull, so have a piece already out.

Now you are ready to start. Take the glue brush in your right hand and make sure that you clean it of excess glue, a job made easier by having a piece of stout wire stretched across the middle of the glue pot. If the glue is a little too thick to spread easily, dip the brush in the hot water in the outside pot, giving it a further scrape on the wire afterwards. Having achieved the right quantity and consistency of glue on the brush, spread it evenly up and down the spine of the book, covering the entire area from top to bottom. Take the piece of mull and place it on the glued surface, making sure that it has an equal amount of flap on either side of the spine (see fig. 17) then give the spine a brisk rub with the folder. A further coat of glue is necessary to attach the piece of wrapping paper on top of the mull. Although the mull does not reach the very top and bottom of the spine the paper does and should, in fact, extend over each end, this extension being trimmed off with shears.

Now take the book out of the press and put the flaps of the mull underneath the boards, the book being then replaced in the press. It will now be ready to have its strip of hollow cut. This is a thin piece of card, strawboard or manilla which is used to stiffen the spine into just the right shape; in fact the spine will take on the shape of the card you cut, so make sure that you get it right.

The average size book should have approximately $\frac{1}{16}$ " overlap on either side of the spine and will be exactly the same height as either of the boards, *not* the spine, which is shorter. The book is now ready for rebacking, a description of which process will follow in the next chapter.

Cloth books, where the old endpapers are to be saved, have a slightly different treatment. This type of rebacking depends for strength on being attached to the spine, whereas the type just described is much stronger. Its additional strength lies not only in attachment to the spine by means of the mull, but the mull is also attached to the boards under the new endpapers. Moreover, the rebacking cloth is attached to the top of the board, thus giving greater strength and firmness all round.

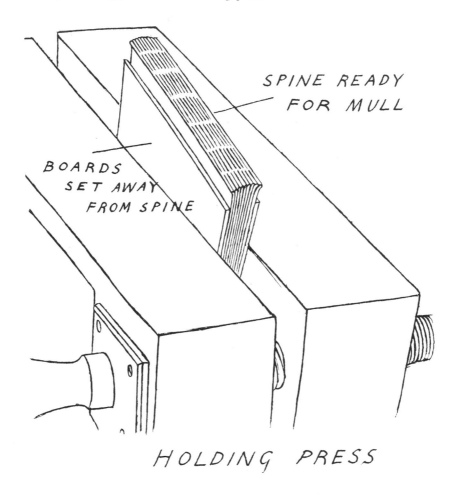

SPINE READY
FOR MULL

BOARDS
SET AWAY
FROM SPINE

HOLDING PRESS

Phillip's Hollow

We take up our alternative method after the new mull has been
attached. You now need a piece of card or manilla cut exactly the
width of the spine. This is easily done by cutting your card to a
straight line and then laying that line on one edge of the spine.
Bend the card over the spine till you come to the other edge where
a further mark is made, this being the exact width of the spine. The
height of the strip will be the same as the mull and when ready the
strip is placed on the spine and the two flaps of the mull brought
over and round it. Ideally, the two pieces of mull should meet in

the centre of the back strip; if they overlap you should trim them to the right size (fig. 18).

The two flaps may then be glued onto the back strip, which will form a hollow when the book is opened. This device is called the Phillip's hollow.

You will still require the outer strip of card as in the previous reback, this being attached to the cloth which in turn will be attached to the Phillip's hollow.

18 Gluing on Phillip's hollow in holding press

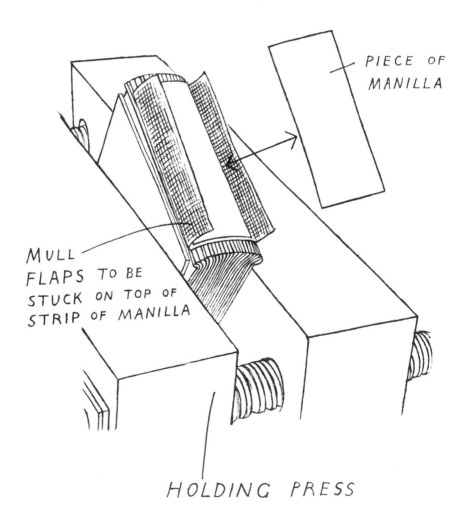

PIECE OF MANILLA

MULL FLAPS TO BE STUCK ON TOP OF STRIP OF MANILLA

HOLDING PRESS

Three fold hollow

There is a further type of hollow, known as the three fold hollow which is used for leather books. To make it you need a thin manilla or similar material. Try and find the grain of the material you use by bending it. It will bend more easily the way the grain runs and the cross grain will resist. The grain should run up the spine so cut your piece of manilla that way. First you need a neat cut edge, so take a knife and cut down the grain to give a straight edge. Now mark the exact width of the book, just as you did in the cloth preparation, but do not cut down the mark. Instead you should score along the marks with a folder, afterwards doubling the manilla over on itself. This then gives you a piece of manilla (see fig. 19), which is ready for gluing. Once again spread a thin coat of glue over the spine, making sure you cover *all* the spine, then place the doubled manilla on the left edge of the spine (fig. 20). The edge of the spine and the manilla should form one straight line. Once this has been achieved it should be rubbed hard with the folder to make sure it sticks in that position. Spread the manilla across the spine to the other edge, using the folder to make it stick down. If you have used too much glue it will begin to squeeze out

19 *Three fold hollow: cutting*

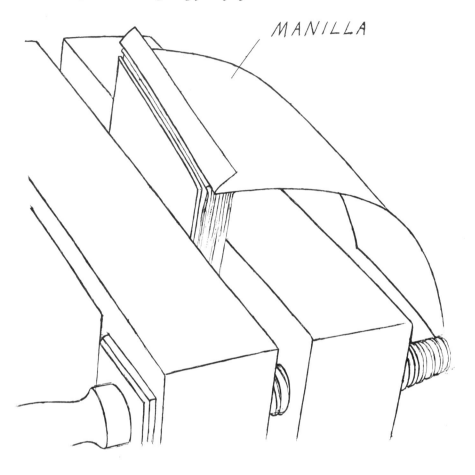

MANILLA

HOLDING PRESS

at this stage; if too little, the hollow will not stick at all. You should now have a situation where the manilla is sticking to the book with a small flap on your left (the piece you measured first) and a larger flap to the right. Carefully bend the large flap to the left, press the manilla along the right hand edge of the spine. You should now see the wisdom of having the grain running up and down the spine, for it will be much easier to fold along the grain. The smaller flap should now have a very thin strip of glue spread on its outer edge so that it will just stick to the inside of the hollow

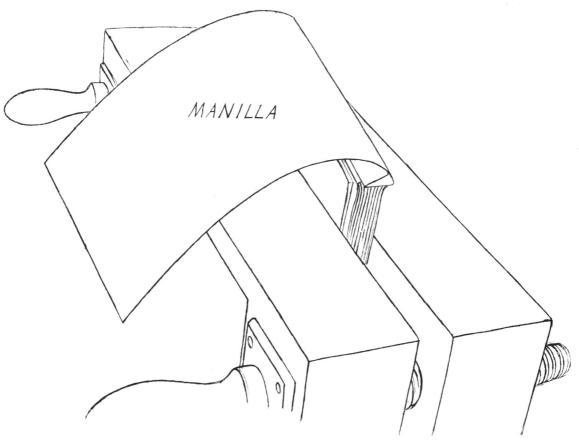

(fig. 21). Rub it down with the folder and then glue the whole back of the hollow, which will have the larger flap stuck to it. You should have an excess of manilla sticking out to your left. This should be folded along that edge of the spine and cut off with a paper knife (fig. 22). Rub the hollow all over the back, especially along each edge where it is most prone to come up. The hollow should be neat, without glue spreading everywhere and should be an exact fit of the spine. The only place it will not be fitting is the head and tail which will have an excess of hollow. Take the shears

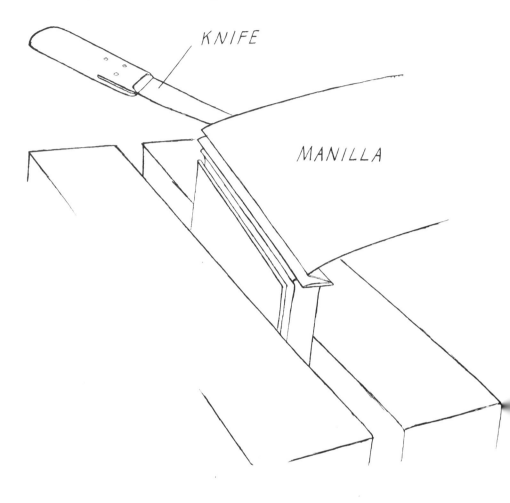

and cut the manilla off with the back of the book in the palm of your hand; this enables you to see the headband that is attached to the top or tail of the spine. The hollow should finish so that it just covers the headband which it protects.

Taking your paper knife or paring knife (fig. 23) make a small cut along each edge of the hollow. If you open the book in the middle (make sure your hands are free of glue first) you will see the hollow open out, which will enable you to insert your knife. Then make a cut of approximately 1″ along the edge of the hollow,

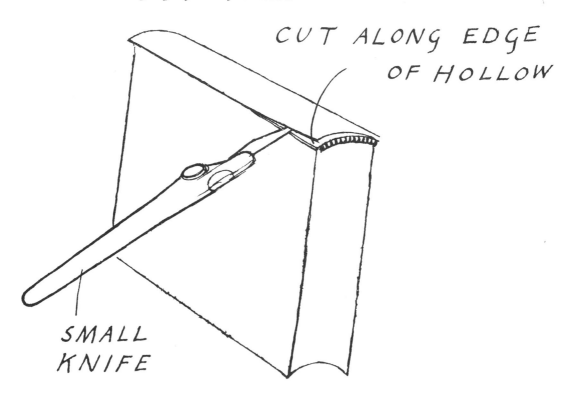

which will allow the material for rebacking to be inserted. The hollow is now completed and you can see how it gets its name. The first fold is in the middle, the second is stuck to the spine and the third is stuck on top of the middle one. I have seen people make up the complete hollow and then stick it on, but it is rather like getting a suit off the peg; made to measure is better and although it is probably more difficult and takes longer, it should always be a good fit.

Raised bands

You may find that on some rebacks you require raised bands and I will now describe how these are made. The raised band was not originally for decoration, as it often is now, but because before 1700 the bookbinder had no choice in the matter, due to the fact that books in those days were sewn either onto heavy cord, strips of leather or vellum. These protuberances stuck out at the back of the book, some of them being quite large, and when the leather was put on they were of course still there, so the leather was moulded round them which not only gave raised bands but also tight backs.

In the nineteenth century the hollow back, which I have just described, became very popular, but before this could happen there had to be a way of getting rid of those natural raised bands formed by the sewing. This was achieved by inserting the cords, onto which the book is sewn, in the book itself by making small cuts; the back of the book thus became smooth and so it became possible to apply the three fold hollow. The original method of sewing, however, does still have its devotees and in some ways they are quite right, but more of that later.

To achieve your false raised bands you will need the following materials and tools: press to hold the book, glue pot containing thinnish glue, shears, pair of dividers, ball point or felt tip pen, some string or strips of leather, depending on the sort of bands you require. String gives normal high bands; leather or thin board will give flatter, wider bands. It is customary to have five bands on most books until you reach the very large folio volumes, which may have six or even seven.

To find out how and where to place your bands you will need to use a pair of dividers so that the spaces between the bands are equal. Try to guess just how much each space will be and then set the dividers to that gap. Starting at the top of the book (fig. 24) lightly mark off your five bands, which should finish looking something like the diagram. Make sure your last space is a quarter larger than the others. This will look right when the book is finished. It is very curious but if the bottom gap is left the same as the others it appears that it is smaller, probably due to the fact that it is nearest the surface the book is standing on. (The same illusions apply to a picture in a mount.) Once having achieved the right places for your bands mark those places as shown again, in the diagram with either a ball point or felt tip pen so that you may see the marks when you have glued the back. Pencil may disappear so do not use it. The next step is to get your string or leather ready for attaching. For this purpose we will assume that you are going to use string, the usual material for bands. If you are

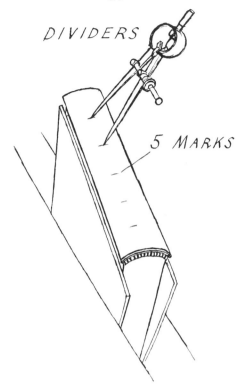

24 *Marking for raised bands*

DIVIDERS

5 MARKS

proficient with string the leather strips will pose no problems. So, taking five strips of string, spread them across the back of the book in order to see the length needed (fig. 25).

When you have the length right keep a firm grip of the string with the left hand and taking the glue brush in your right put the string on the edge of the pot, placing the brush on top, and then pull the string through to get a nice sticky coat of glue on the string. Do this several times, making sure that all the string is covered, but not smothered, as you do not want lumpy bands.

Keep hold of the string, give the brush a quick wash in hot water and after scraping the excess water and glue off the brush give the hollow a smooth thin coat of glue all over. Then replace the brush in the pot. Drape the string over the tail of the hollow and, taking the shears, cut off the correct length. This should allow plenty of room to grasp the pieces of string with either hand and

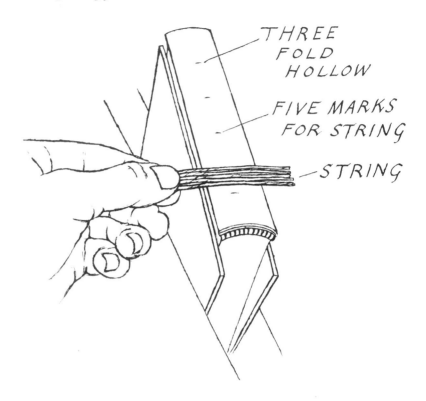

THREE FOLD HOLLOW

FIVE MARKS FOR STRING

STRING

place them on their five marks (fig. 26). If you want to be fussy you may measure the gaps again with the dividers after the strings have been put on, but if you have made your marks correctly and placed the strings on them, they should be spaced well enough (fig. 27). Later, when the glue is dry, you may cut away the overlapping string with your paring knife. Your book is now hollowed, banded and ready for its new leather.

Headbands

There is one other item which should be mentioned at this time — headbands. You may find that these are missing when you come to repair or reback a book. Generally speaking, it is only leather-bound books which have headbands, although they are not unknown in cloth books. Headbands should be sewn onto the book, as you will see if you have a leather book with the back off, exposing the headband. This is quite a tricky operation, and you may get round

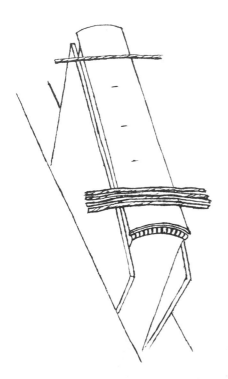
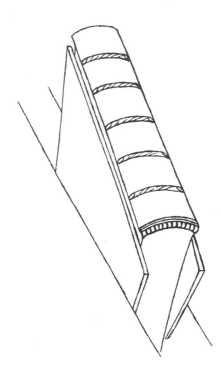

it by buying made-up headbands which are quite reasonable and, although they do not approach the real thing, are adequate for many jobs. However, for those who like to do the work themselves, this is how a headband is made. You will need coloured silks, specially made for the purpose, a needle, shears and some leather and vellum which has been stuck together to form a pliable base for the headband to be sewn onto.

A strip slightly less than the square of the book should be cut from the leather and vellum. That is to say, the gap between the book and the edge of the board. You should have a strip that is a good bit longer than you need, to give plenty of room to work with. Your silk will need to be of two colours. Often yellow is used with another colour that matches the leather. On occasions white is preferred, but I think yellow is eminently suitable and nearly always use it myself. Basically you need white, yellow, green, scarlet, claret, brown, blue and black. Assuming that you have

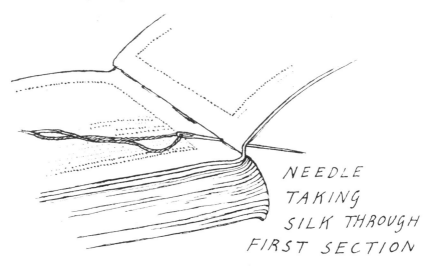

NEEDLE TAKING SILK THROUGH FIRST SECTION

your two silks and your strip to sew into, you will first have to thread one of the silks through the needle which should pass through the middle of the first section (fig. 28), leaving one end at the top and one coming through the spine of the book, which is knotted to the other piece of silk and the knot pulled back tight to the book which may be placed in a small press leaving both hands free. You will need them!

Have the fore edge of the book facing you when you put the book in the press, placing the strip of vellum, which should be slightly curved to match the curve of the back, along the rounded edge at the top or bottom of the spine, whichever you are doing. Taking the length of silk from the inside of the book make two turns round the strip (fig. 29) followed by two turns with the other silk giving alternate colours. Make sure both silks are wound the same way, starting from behind the strip, then bringing the silk towards you and going under the strip, then repeating the process. Before starting your second length of silk bring it across the first length, giving a neat hitch after every two, or if you prefer three, turns. So, basically, the method is to wind a run of one colour, then pass the second colour in a hitch over the first strand, more turns then the first strand again, repeating till you reach the middle of the book. Here you should take one of the strands through a section of the book again, anchoring the headband in the middle as well as on

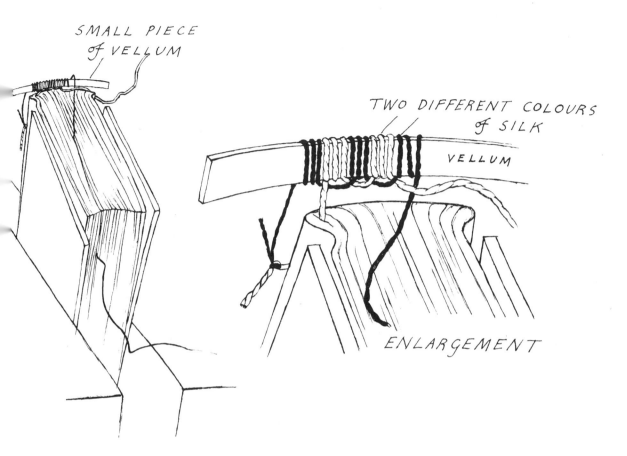

SMALL PIECE
of VELLUM

TWO DIFFERENT COLOURS
of SILK

VELLUM

ENLARGEMENT

both sides, finally tying off in the same way as you started. When you attach your three fold hollow, the headband will nestle into it and form a strong and attractive finish to the top and tail of the book.

4 Rebacking in cloth and leather

In the previous chapters, everything has been prepared for the number one repairing job, rebacking. We will now assume that your book is ready for the actual reback. I shall describe in the following order rebacking of cloth, paper and leather volumes.

Cloth

The cloth and paper rebacks must fall into two separate parts, those with new endpapers and those with Phillip's hollows. In the first instance it is much easier to perform the work, because after the new cloth has been put on the case may be removed from the book and worked on separately. However, first you should have your cloth volume lifted inside and out, your piece of matching cloth for the repair and a strip of card or manilla for the new spine. The tools to have handy are shears and folder, with either paste or glue for the adhesive. Paste is much easier for the beginner as it does not dry as quickly as glue but as it soaks through it does have the disadvantage of making the cloth rather soggy, so use glue if you can.

To start the reback you should square the boards, that is to say, make sure the boards which form the case are equally spaced from the book all round and also equal with each other. Paste or glue your strip of cloth, placing the card for the hollow in the exact centre (fig. 30). Paste the board where the original cloth has been lifted as this will be rather dry, then you are ready to apply the new cloth to the binding. Take the glued, or pasted, cloth and attach one side (fig. 31) to the board, taking care not to move the board from its square. You should remember that the strip of card which you placed in the middle of the cloth should be in the middle of the spine so, as you stick the other side of the cloth down, check to see this is correct. Check also the head and tail to make sure the length is right too. The strip of hollow should extend exactly the same length as the boards which will stiffen the weakest place in the binding, the head and tail. When you have correctly positioned your cloth rub down the sides to ensure that it stays that way. Having done this you may take the book out of its case. You should now have the inside of the case face up and will proceed to turn in the ends (fig. 32). If at this time you notice that the hollow strip is not

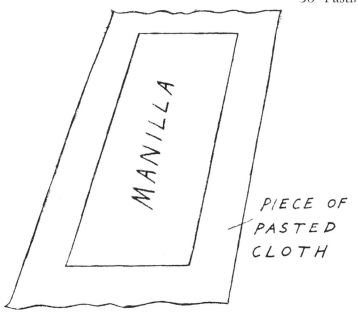

30 Pasting cloth for reback

MANILLA

PIECE OF
PASTED
CLOTH

31 Attaching new cloth to spine

MANILLA

CLOTH

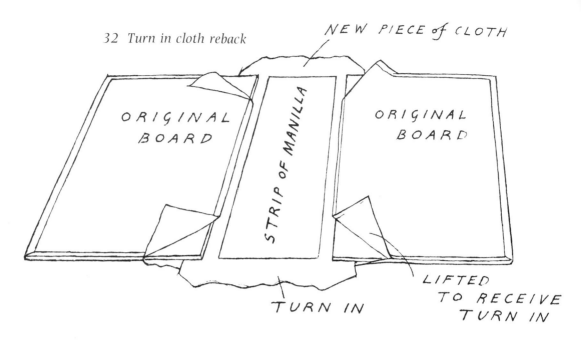

32 Turn in cloth reback

NEW PIECE of CLOTH

ORIGINAL BOARD

STRIP OF MANILLA

ORIGINAL BOARD

TURN IN

LIFTED TO RECEIVE TURN IN

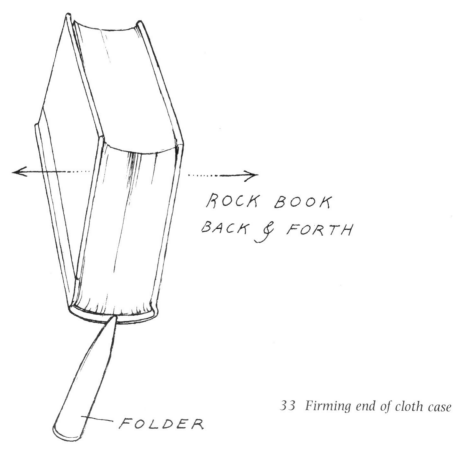

ROCK BOOK BACK & FORTH

33 Firming end of cloth case

FOLDER

in the middle take it out before the glue dries and replace it more exactly. When you are turning in the cloth be careful to see that there are no 'pencil cases'. This is a term we use in the trade to denote that the turn in has not been pulled tight to the board or hollow, leaving enough space to slide a pencil in. I may say this can happen all too easily if you are hurrying to finish before the glue dries, but better take your time and have to put on a little more glue than find you have a dreaded 'pencil case'.

When you have turned in both ends of the cloth you may return the book to the case, making sure that the cloth is stuck all round and giving the new back a good rub with the folder. The head and tail will need to be shaped to match the 'round' of the book. This can easily be done by using the folder point, which is inserted in between the book and the hollow; then pressing the folder down, you rock the book back and forth to shape the new back (fig. 33).

This should leave you with a completed reback which will need an hour or two to dry – double this time if you have used paste. If you have several cloth rebacks to do, it is wise to prepare them all first, so as to give each one time to dry. Then, having finished the last one, you may return to the first which should now be ready to have the old sides put down.

First trim away the rough edge of the old cloth so that you have a nice straight edge; this will be done by using a very sharp knife, a metal rule and a piece of thin board to cut on. Slip your piece of board under the cloth, lay the rule on top and holding the book firmly with the left hand, run the knife down the edge of the rule, cutting off the rough edge.

To lay down the old cloth sides, both inside and out, you should use paste, *not* glue. But remember, a little goes a long way, or you will find the paste squeezing out like toothpaste out of a tube.

The insides should be stuck first, followed by the outsides, not forgetting to put in some greaseproof paper to protect the book from the damp paste.

The pasting down of the outsides is pretty simple if common sense is used. Just cover the surfaces of the board and cloth with enough paste to make them wet, then gently smooth down the old cloth, leaving no bubbles or bumps and paying special attention to the edges of the boards where you first make your incision for lifting the cloth.

Give the pasted down cloth a light wipe with some moist cotton wool, but do not scrub at it or you will remove the texture and colour. If the book has an old back that you wish to preserve, trim round it to make it neat then paste it on the inside and stick it to the new spine.

Paper

Having completed the cloth reback we now come to the paper binding or, as it is termed in the trade 'book in boards'. This was quite a common binding in the nineteenth century when many volumes were published with this type of binding. It was looked upon as a cheap, temporary job, it being expected that the purchaser would replace the boards with a handsome binding of his own choice. However, as most people know, many of these volumes are still to be found in their original bindings and very fragile they are too. Basically they are made up of thickish paper mainly in grey, white and blue; sometimes two colours are used. The spine is generally double lined, but this was the only strengthening that was used. Unfortunately, in my opinion, the preservation of this type of binding has become desirable to book collectors who wish to preserve a book in its original case, even though it is most unsuitable to do so, and is largely a waste of time, as these bindings were never intended to last.

These repairs are most difficult to complete satisfactorily and I would not advise the beginner to tackle one until he has completed many cloth rebacks to a good standard. Basically, the job is similar, but paper is, of course, very fragile and the slightest mistake results in a tear. In fact the whole lifting process can develop into a series of tears and cuts. It is possible to reback straight over the top of the old paper, but in my opinion this is a last resort and amounts to saying that the job has beaten you. The main thing to do with a paper reback is to strengthen it with linen, which is put underneath the paper being used for the reback. Linen is used because it is pretty thin, but very strong and to all outward signs the repair has been made solely with paper. The paper repair is also tricky from

52

the point of materials because this type of paper is rather difficult to find. I have found that my paper has had to be saved and scrounged from various sources, mainly from old wrapping paper. If you intend to do many repairs to books you will need to cultivate this magpie habit. Collections of various old papers and cloths are most useful and cannot be purchased from a shop.

Most books in paper boards have thin paper lettering labels which should be carefully preserved and replaced on the new back, as these are impossible to reproduce exactly.

The skilful reback in paper is a delight to see, for it is possible to complete the rebacking so that it is almost invisible. This is easiest when the book to be rebacked is one of those that has two colours, the first being the spine and the second the side paper. The spine paper is carefully removed and the new paper slipped under the old side paper which, when replaced undamaged, will show no signs of repair, especially when the old label has been replaced. If at some time you are able to complete a job of this kind with no mistakes, the finished article will give you a great deal of satisfaction as will any invisible repair or reback.

Leather
The third item on our rebacking list is the leather reback. Although more varied this job can be easier than the other two once a little confidence has been acquired. The reason for this is that leather is very pliable when wet, which allows you to take your time to complete the reback.

The main problems for the beginner are (1) staining the leather the correct colour (2) paring it to the right thinness. The paring of leather, as mentioned in chapter 1, is a big stumbling block, but if the beginner persists he or she should manage to pare the leather thin enough to enable the reback to be made, and steady repetition of the job over a period of time will soon bring skill.

The reback may be started when you have completed the staining and paring of the leather, and the lifting of the old leather. Again, there are the two types of reback, hollow and tight backs, which are then again split into a further two, plain spines and those with raised bands.

Firstly, the plain spine with a three fold hollow. This reback will be started by moistening the new piece of leather with some wet cotton wool and then pasting it well on the inside. You should also paste the boards and the hollow just enough to wet the surfaces, after which you may apply the new leather to the hollow, trying to get an equal amount of leather on both sides. Then press the flaps down on to the boards (fig. 34), stretching the leather tight across the back. Once you have the leather sticking along the spine and both boards you may take your folder and smooth the leather along the boards, removing any excess paste that may squeeze out as a result. You are now ready for the turning in of the ends, which is a very similar job to the cloth turn in and, in fact, should be easier. You might have to put a little more paste on the leather to be turned and also on the dry board, where the leather will go. Your position for starting this job should be as shown in diagram 7, with the corners of the turn in so that they match the shape of the lifted area. Now, as you turn the leather in, it should slip in to the gap between the folds of the hollow then up the cuts you made in the same. You will have to learn to do all this with one hand while the other holds the book itself. The palette knife is often very handy to push the leather in, used like an extension of your finger. Having turned both ends in, check each board (fig. 35), making sure the leather is tight on the turn in (no 'pencil cases') and that the board is just nipping the leather between itself and the hollow. The headcaps come next and you may find you have not enough leather to cover them properly. Should this be the case then pull some more out using finger and thumb but try to achieve this without opening the book or you may disturb the turn in. (This operation was described in chapter 1.)

To finish the job, give all the new leather a light wash with damp cotton wool to remove any excess paste, then put some strips of greaseproof paper inside to protect the book and leave to dry, making sure that the part of the book that has been rebacked, the spine, is not touching anything, this being most easily done by resting the book on the edge of a table with the repair sticking out over the edge. The tight back reback with no raised bands is exactly the same job except that when you turn the leather in, it is

34 Fitting new leather to spine

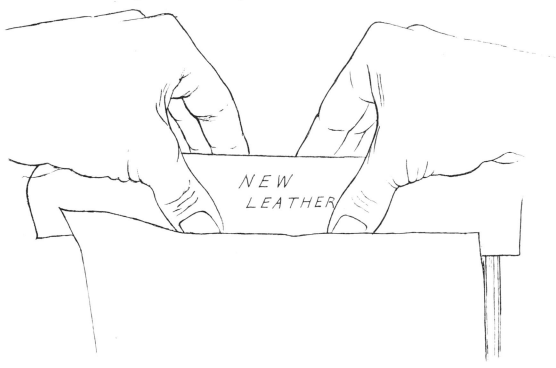

NEW LEATHER

35 Tightening leather turn in

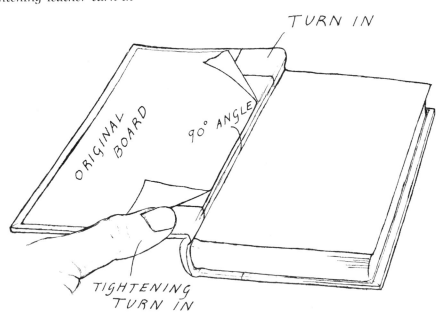

TURN IN

ORIGINAL BOARD

90° ANGLE

TIGHTENING TURN IN

turned under itself, you should make sure that the piece of leather you turn in under the spine is pasted on both sides.

The book with raised bands, be it hollow or tight back, will have the same treatment. When you have pasted all the surfaces as you did for the plain spines place the leather on the back as before. Now here is the difference, you must allow extra leather for the raised bands, the bigger the book the more leather is needed. Starting at the middle band push the leather down around the band and onto the boards, following this with the bands on either side of the middle one, and lastly by the outside bands. Using the folder, make sure that the leather is stuck to the boards on both sides as this will keep it in the right place. Having assured this take your band nippers and again starting at the middle band nip gently but firmly along the band, moulding the leather into the right shape. The other bands should follow just as before, but watch to see if, when you nip one band, the leather pulls away from the band you have just nipped, as it sometimes does. If this happens the answer is clear, you have not pushed enough leather round the bands when you first started, so this must be remedied by pushing some more in towards the middle from either end. Once all the bands have been nipped it is often beneficial to press down the spaces between the band with a rule, using one edge flush against a band. The rest of the job is as before.

In half and quarter leather rebacks there is often very little leather on the boards before you come to paper or cloth. In this situation it is usually best to remove all the old leather and take the new right up to and under the cloth or paper, giving a very neat repair, as long as you are careful not to damage the paper or cloth. It is quite common, in fact, when repairing a half leather book to remove all the leather, corners as well, and renew them, to give the appearance of an old book in good condition. This idea is not so much to deceive as to keep what one can of the original binding rather than rebinding with all new materials. Some books have interesting marbled side and endpapers which would be lost if the book were rebound, not to mention the saving of some costly materials.

5 Disbanding, resewing, trimming edges

In this chapter we begin to tackle basic rebinding which starts with the book having to be resewn.

A book is made up of sections which in their turn are made up of double pages. That is to say, one double page comprises two leaves or four numbered pages. These leaves will not be numbered consecutively i.e. 1, 2, 3, 4 as nearly always there are eight or more pages to a section. This would give pages 1 and 8 front and back with pages 3 to 6 in the middle. Quite often you will find that sections are made up of twelve or sixteen pages, but always the first and last pages are joined together followed by the second and penultimate etc. This gives the section its strength, at the same time forming the book into so many sections. You may happen on a volume that is uncut or unopened as it is sometimes termed. This will show you how the section was printed on a large piece of paper which was then folded into the section, but as the book was not trimmed the pages are still as they were folded. There are names for the sizes of these pieces of paper but I do not intend to go into that here (see glossary).

Disbinding

To return to our resewing, I will explain how you should pull a book so that the sections are separated. This is a tricky operation if you are not sure how many pages made a section and I have seen books pulled with many pages torn due to a beginner separating the sections at the wrong places.

Every section will have a letter or number telling you where the section starts, and most books use the alphabet starting of course with A. You will find this letter at the bottom of the pages on your left as you look at the page. If you start at the beginning of the book the first few pages may be numbered thus, i, ii, iii etc. in the same place; you will eventually come to the letter A which will be followed on the next page by ai then aii. If you continue to look at each page you will come to B and by counting the pages between A and B you will discover the number of pages in a section.

If the book is large, having more than 26 sections, the alphabet will run out necessitating a new start which is done by the following Aa, Bb etc. or AA, BB. Quite often it is possible to see where the sections start and finish as the glue has dried and fallen away from the spine leaving the sections separated except for what sewing thread is left. When this is the case you will find it much quicker to just cut any thread between the sections thus separating them quickly, afterwards going through them again to remove the old thread which is running down the middle of each section.

If the book you are pulling is of the tight back variety with raised bands, it is often possible to cut off the bands which will also assist in the separating of the sections. All dismantling or pulling of books should be carried out with care, for a ripped section can easily occur, and is usually the result of a string in the middle of the section that has been overlooked. Naturally, if you attempt to separate one section from another without cutting the strings first the pages will tear.

Having removed all the string from your sections the book is ready for resewing but two things may be necessary first.

Pressing

If the book has small sections, e.g. eight pages, or is very fat it would be desirable to squash it down a bit before sewing. The general idea is to get out some of the air which seems to puff a book up after it has been pulled and to do this a nipping press is used. The book is placed between two boards and then put into the middle of the press whereupon the platen is screwed down tight, compressing the book. There are various types of nipping press, so it is not strictly necessary to have a metal one, as in the photographs, although this is of course the best.

Sawing

Leave the book in the press for an hour or two then, when it is removed, you will find it compact and ready for sawing. Some books have perfectly adequate saw marks which were used to sew the book originally, but often the saw marks are much too big and deep, making new ones desirable.

This is the way to make your new saw marks. First you must be sure that the book is square, which is done by tapping the whole book against a flat surface on the back and head, then place the

37 *Large nipping press*

book in either a lying or holding press using a couple of boards on either side of the book to protect it. Once it is firmly gripped in the press you can make your saw marks. With small and average sized books you only need three main cuts, with two tie cuts (fig. 38). As you can see from the diagram the cuts go straight across the book, and the three main ones are where the cords will go that the book will be sewn round. If the book is a large one you may need more marks, the usual number being five with, again, one either end for the kettle stitches. Generally speaking, leather books have five cuts, as this number matches the normal number of bands on the spine. Cloth books seldom have more than four.

The point of the five cuts and five bands is clear when the book is finished as the raised bands conceal the sewing strings making for a neater job. Therefore, if you are sewing a book to be bound in leather with raised bands, you should mark out their position carefully with dividers, as you did when placing your false bands on the three fold hollow.

When you have drawn lines across the spine of the book with a pencil you may take your tenon saw and make the cuts. These cuts should be just deep enough to cut through to the middle of each section. If you are in any doubt you should take note of how many pages are in each section as this will give you a very good notion of how deep to go. The eight-page section will not need a very deep cut, but some of the twentieth-century cloth books have quite thick sections needing a much deeper cut.

When you start to make a cut it is much easier to pull the saw back towards you to start with, then, having done this several times, you may then be able to move the saw back and forth in the normal way. If you try to move the saw forward from the start you will find it difficult and may damage the book. When you have made all the cuts remove the book and just check to see that they have come through to the middle of each section. You will find sewing extremely difficult if the cuts do not reach the middle of the section.

For those readers who have very old leather books that need resewing, the following advise is useful. It is customary with the latter not to saw the book at all, but rather to resew it in the

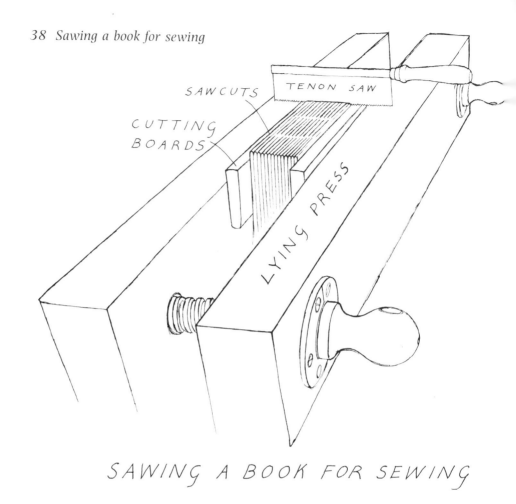

SAWCUTS

TENON SAW

CUTTING BOARDS

LYING PRESS

SAWING A BOOK FOR SEWING

original way with fixed raised bands. This entails sewing the book with the strings protruding from the spine, which also necessitates a fixed or tight back book.

I think you will be interested to see, should you complete both types of sewing, that the book that is sewn with the string pulled in to the saw marks will not be so easy to open and read as will be the book that is sewn onto strings that protrude.

While the latter book is easier to open it loses much of its advantage as the leather must be applied in the tight back way. So the choice is yours. Personally, I think that books that are dated before 1700 should be bound in their original way whenever possible.

Sewing

To return to the sewing, we now come to the job itself, which requires the use of the sewing press or jig. This item (fig. 39) can be pretty expensive so if possible I would advise you to make do with a self-made one or get someone handy to make one for you. The main idea is to follow the shape of the original but simplify it somewhat. You will need a flat smooth piece of wood 20″ × 12″ × 1″, and three other suitable pieces to form the uprights and the top (fig. 40). Two pieces of wood should also be nailed underneath the flat piece at either end to raise it slightly, again, as with the original. What you will not have is the adjustable bar to tighten the strings so this job will have to be done in another way which I will explain shortly.

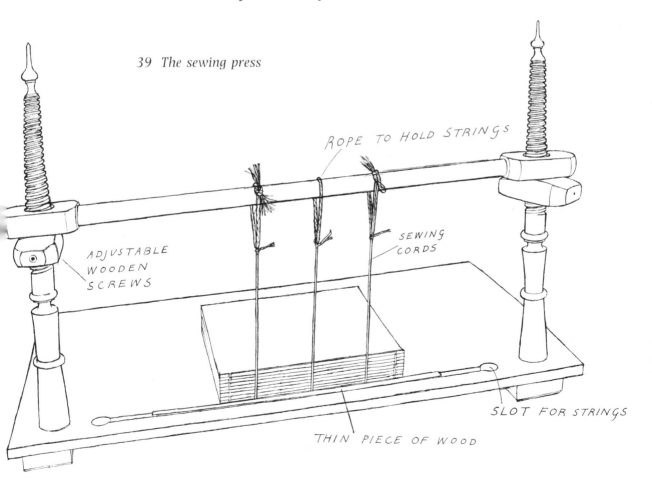

39 The sewing press

ROPE TO HOLD STRINGS

ADJUSTABLE WOODEN SCREWS

SEWING CORDS

SLOT FOR STRINGS

THIN PIECE OF WOOD

The other items you must have are sewing thread (button thread is a good substitute), sewing cord or string, a large needle, sewing keys and some drawing pins. Both the sewing thread and cord may be purchased from book-binding suppliers, but good sewing cord is becoming difficult to obtain. It looks rather like ordinary string, but in fact is very different. The individual strands of the cords, usually six, will separate from each other very easily. This enables the string to be fluffed out which becomes important when you wish to thread it through a board. If you try to separate the strands of any cheap piece of string you will find this either very difficult or the string will disintegrate.

I will first describe how to set up an ordinary sewing press for those lucky enough to have one.

The press should be on the table in front of you with the tall arms nearest you. The adjustable bar should be well above the book you intend to sew, and should have at least five circles of tape round it. These tapes are the places to attach your strings to and we will assume that there are three. When you attach a piece of sewing cord you will need a key to lock it under the press. The cord should not be cut from its reel until it is secured as it is difficult to judge just how much is needed. So, having attached the cord to the tape, take a key and start to wind the cord round it

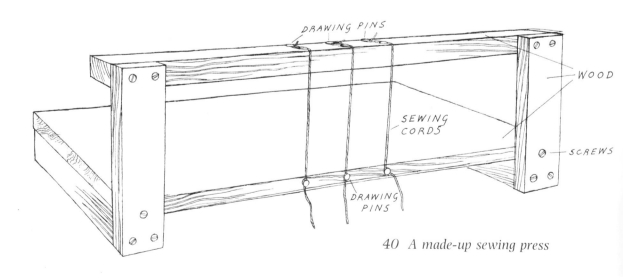

40 A made-up sewing press

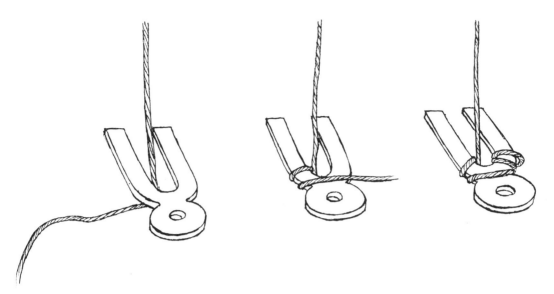

(fig. 41). The key is placed partly underneath the bottom of the press to enable all the cords to be kept at about the same tautness. Once the cord has been wound around the key far enough to keep it there, slip it through the long slit in the base of the press, then twist it so that it sits flat underneath. If you have wound it correctly the cord should be just taut; then follow the first with the two others. If you place the book on the press with the back facing you, it should be very easy to slide the keys around until all three cords are in line with the three cuts in the book. This is the time to screw up the bar, which tightens the cords and keeps the sewing firm. Be careful not to tighten the bar adjusters so that the cords snap; it is all too easy to do this. You need the cords just tight enough to keep the sewing firm.

So now you have your sewing press with its cords in the right places and nicely tight. You may start to sew the book from either end, but I, personally, like to start at the back and finish with the front. Therefore the book should be turned upside down and you take the last section of the book and place it on the press with the top to your left. Take trouble to see that this is done correctly or you may find you have sewn the book upside down. Take your needle and thread it with the sewing thread, giving yourself about 5 or 6 lengths of a section before cutting it. You will find that after a time there is a standard length that is best for you when sewing and only trial and error will find it. The sewing is begun like this: (fig. 42) push the needle through the first hole in the section on your extreme right using your left hand to hold the section open in the middle, then pull the needle through and bring it back through the second hole, but make sure that it is on the right hand side of the first cord. You may find you have to peer over the top of the press to see what to do on the other side, but if your saw cuts were made in the right way you will soon learn to find the holes without looking.

The needle should now be pushed back through the second hole but on the other side of the cord, thus catching and holding the cord. Pull the needle through from the other side again and this time also pull the extra thread till all you have is a few inches left sticking out of the first hole. You then repeat the operation for the second cord as with the first, threading out on the right, then back in again on the left going round the third cord and doing that in the same way. Finally you come out through the last hole on your left

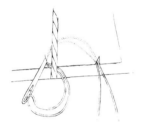

42 *Starting to sew a book*

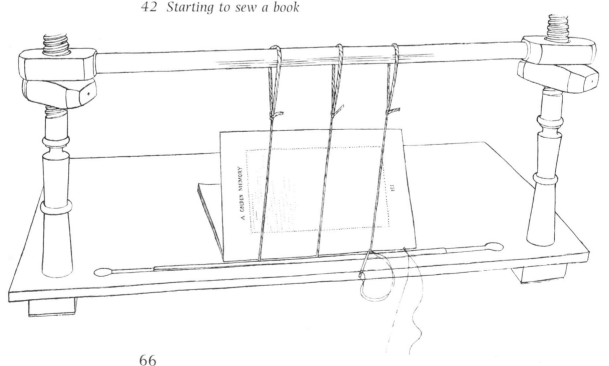

and you are ready to attach a second section. Be careful to place it on the press in the same way as the first, then opening it in the middle and holding it with your left hand again start the process just described in reverse; work back to where you began on the first section. When you reach the spot make sure that you have pulled the sewing thread tight all through both sections and also that the second section sits exactly on top of the first. The thread should always be pulled tight in the direction in which you are sewing or you will cut the section. You must ensure that every section is level with the previous one and as you finish a section press it down on either side of the cords so as to keep as much swelling and air out of the book as possible. When you start to sew on the third section catch in the piece of thread that was left sticking out of the first section where you started. You should continue to catch in this strand until it has ended or the book is finished. On reaching the end of the third section and before starting the fourth, you must hitch the sections together. This is done by passing the needle and thread in between (fig. 43) the first two sections around the joining point and back, forming a knot which will keep the sewing firm. This hitch knot (known as the kettle stitch) is performed at each end; once you have three sections and on completion of the

43 *Making a kettle stitch*

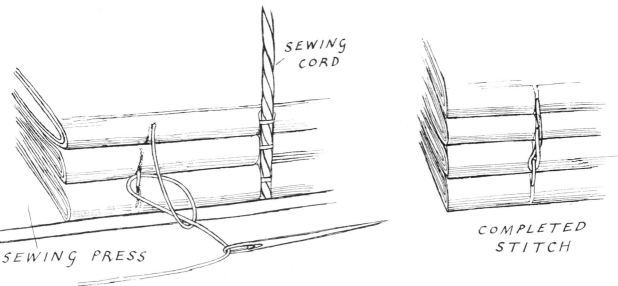

last section a double hitch is made to tie off and finish the sewing. Before you make any hitch knot be careful to keep all the sewing pulled tight, because it is not much use making the knot if the thread is loose. When the book is all sewn together it is a simple matter to cut the strings close to the tapes and then take out and unwind the keys.

If you are going to use the made up sewing press the sewing procedure is exactly the same, but as you have no screw adjustment and no place to put your keys, other arrangements must be made. You can use the pieces of tape of course, and to attach your cords at the bottom drawing pins are quite satisfactory. It is best to get the heavier type of drawing pin because these do not bend so easily and you do have to put a bit of pressure on them to pull the cord tight. If you place your book on the press in the middle, as before, you can fix each cord in just the right place. Remember once they are fixed with drawing pins they cannot be moved as with the other press. The drawing pin is pushed three quarters in then the cord is taken round it pulling hard to keep it tight then winding several times round it to maintain the tension, if necessary placing a further pin below the first for further turns. Give both pins a tap with a hammer to keep them secure and then fix the other two cords in the same way. This is nowhere near as good as the professional sewing press, but it is a good deal better than none at all.

You may wish to sew on tapes, but I would advise against this for 90% of all sewing. It is a difficult process to perfect and I am convinced that for most purposes the method I have described is best. We do, however, return again to the problem of the much older book which is sewn on to cords that stick out on the spine. When you have sewn a book that has been sawn it will be noticeable that the sewing cords slip snugly into the cuts leaving a smooth spine. With the older type of sewing there are no saw marks but it is quite reasonable to make a pencil mark, so you know where the section should fit on the cords. The cords will number at least five this time and should be doubled. This is easily done by passing the cord through tape thereby doubling it. This doubled cord is rather heavy and is very difficult to fix with drawing pins, although it is possible; unless you have a proper sewing press it is best left alone. When the cords are all fixed and tightened you are again ready to start to thread the sections on. Starting as before pass the needle through the first hole and back through the second one. Now comes the difference, the sewing thread should be wound round and in between the cords in the figure of eight formation (fig. 44). This is quite a slow process, especially when there are over 100 sections which is quite common, but it is most efficient, strong and superior as far as sewing goes to any other method. The rest of the sewing proceeds as before.

44 *Figure-of-8 sewing onto raised cords*

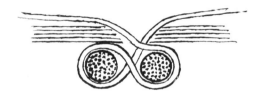

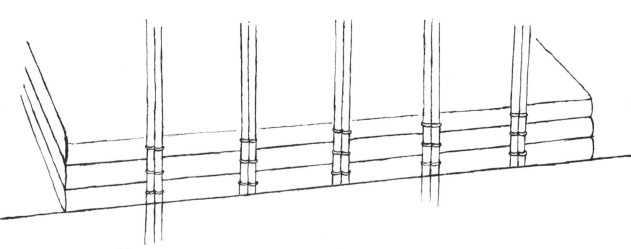

Endpapers

There now comes the problem of endpapers, which can be affixed in several ways depending on their type. The most straightforward way is to take a piece of plain white paper which is twice the size of the book, fold it in half then stick it on to the edge of the first page next to the spine, with a little paste (see fig. 14). The correct method for applying the paste is to cover the endpaper, except for $\frac{1}{8}''$ next to the fold, then spread paste along the uncovered piece, which is carefully placed on the book so that the folded edge of the endpaper is level with the first section of the book. The same applies to the back of the book. You may wish, however, to have more than just the minimum single endpaper, so this is how it is done. You should make sections of your endpapers and sew them on to the book either during the initial sewing process just described, or afterwards, in the case of a book that does not need to be resewn. Instead of having one folded endpaper by itself place a further folded sheet inside the first giving a four leaf section or if you would rather have a six leaf section place a further folded sheet inside the second one. This process is most useful when you have a very thin pamphlet that needs padding out to make it into a respectable book. You can add as many folded, plain paper sections as you think necessary and indeed should you require to make a plain unwritten book for writing or sketching you can do it in this way.

There is an alternative method of sewing on endpapers, which is to wrap the folded end of the paper around the first section. This leaves a small stub in between the first two sections. The endpaper is sewn on when the section is attached during the normal sewing of the book. This method is most commonly used when new cloth books are being bound, although it has been used for many different bindings for many years.

I find it pleasing to have a single endpaper for the actual 'paste down' when I am binding a leather book. Although I may have other endpages sewn on previously I always stick on one folded sheet to act as the final endpaper to be pasted onto the board. This gives a nice clean finish to the inside with no break along the joint which is unavoidable if the endpaper has been sewn on. When you have attached your endpapers, whether by sewing or sticking, they will need to be trimmed to match the size of the book. This job is performed with the rule, paring knife and a piece of board to cut on. The rule is placed inside the endpaper, separating it from the first page and level with the outside of that page. The rule is kept in place by pressing hard down on the book from above with the left hand. You may start at either end of the book but do not trim the fore-edge unless the book is to be rebound or rebacked in cloth. This is because leather books have their endpapers pasted down open, and cloth books are pasted down closed, then put in a nipping press. All edges to be trimmed may be done in this way, turning the book as required. The way to make the cut with the paring knife is to cut towards you remembering not to ease the pressure on the rule until you can see that the endpaper is cut right through. The knife should be kept very sharp for this job, and one cut should finish it. If you find yourself making several strokes with the knife there is a danger of making the cuts in different places. Believe me, it is all too easy to do this, so keep your knives very sharp, but mind your fingers!

Pressing
With your book sewn and endpapered it will now be ready for further pressing. During the sewing, however careful you are, the paper gets all puffed up, especially in the spine. Before pressing the book do ensure that all the sections are level with each other along the spine, and if they are not, several sharp blows with the book on a flat firm surface (fig. 45) may level them out.

If it does not you will have to try and get them level by using a rule in the middle of the section and working it into its proper position. This performance is, of course, unnecessary if the sewing has been done correctly. The book will not press correctly unless every section is level with the one above.

The book is now placed between two smooth clean boards and put in the middle of the nipping press just as it was before the book was sewn. Make sure none of the sewing cords are caught between the boards as this will make a nasty impression on your book. Wring down the press as hard as you can; it should be left for

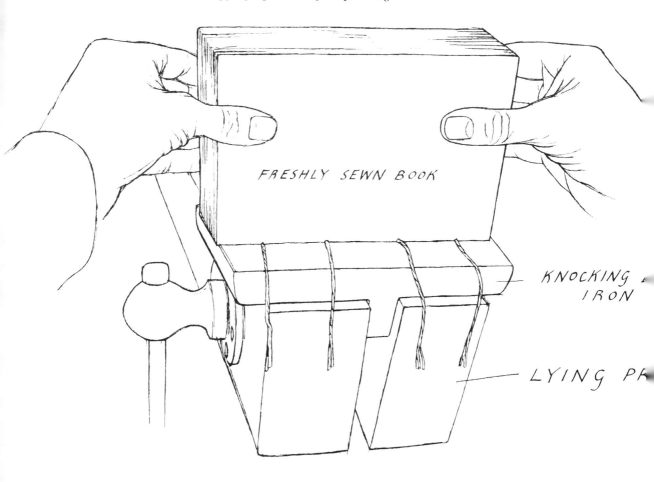

four or five hours at least, overnight would not be too long. When the book is removed from the press you will find that it has squashed down quite a bit, in fact the cords the book was sewn with will now be concertinaed and will need to be pulled tight. Wind a couple of turns of a cord round the pointed end of your folder and pull the slack through till the cord on the far side starts to move, then you have it tight. This will prevent the book from springing back to its original state.

Gluing

The sections of the book, now firm and pressed together, need to be lightly glued before the process of rebinding can begin. The cords should be separated and fluffed so they may be kept dry during the gluing. To separate the sections of the cords roll the cord between two fingers in the opposite way to which it was made and the strands will spring apart. Then separate each strand with the palette knife until you have 5 or 6 separate strands. Taking the palette knife fluff the string using the blunt edge of the knife (fig. 46). When all the cords are fluffy place the book between two boards, leaving the back of the book showing but tucking all the cords under the protection of the two boards so that no glue touches them. To keep everything steady and firm place a heavy weight on the top board. Taking the glue brush, clean off as much glue as you can, then dip it in the hot water of the pot and give it another quick clean whereupon it is ready for the book, so take the

46 Fluffing the sewing cords

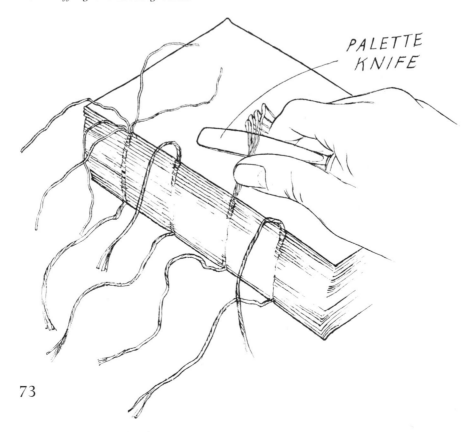

PALETTE
KNIFE

brush and firmly rub it all over the spine of the book. A phrase we have in the trade sums it up well: 'hot and thin, well rubbed in'. You do not want thick, heavy glue on the spine, but just a thin coating to seal the sections, so remember to keep it thin and wipe off any residue with old, crumpled up paper. After gluing remove the boards and wipe off any glue that may have got under them, or onto the endpapers, then leave to dry.

Trimming

There are occasions when it is necessary to trim all the edges of a book. Usually this would apply to modern books; it is most unwise to trim an old book as this could easily diminish its value. Do not therefore, trim a book unless it is unavoidable in which case the best time would be two hours after the sealing process just described.

There are two ways of trimming books, the old way and the new The new way is to guillotine the edges with a machine, but although you may have access to one of these, at a technical college perhaps, they are not things you would buy. There is a method of trimming that I still use on occasions called 'the plough'. The plough is used on the reverse side of the lying press (fig. 48) and is quite an old and rather slow method of trimming a book. Unlike the guillotine the plough cuts each page along its length, whereas the guillotine chops straight through. The plough itself is quite easy to use, but unfortunately there is a slight snag – the fitting of the book into the press.

You must place the book between wooden boards made just for that purpose (see fig. 49) with a thin piece of waste board on the left hand side, which is there to protect the wooden boards from the knife when it cuts the final pages of the book. The front board you will see is slightly lower than the back as this is the part that will be cut off and, in fact, it is as well to mark this with a pencil line that has been made with a set square to keep your cut at 90° to the back of the book. You may then place the front board level with that line and, setting the lying press to the right gap, ease the book and boards into the press until the front board is level with the press itself. This is not easy to do and the beginner will probably

make several attempts before getting the book and both boards in their right places.

If everything is not just so, it is not possible to trim the book and, in fact, it is very easy to make a bad mistake, so don't try to trim the book until the front board is level with the press and the line on the book is level with the cutting boards.

The cutting process is pretty much a formality, as long as the cutting blade is sharp. The plough is moved back and forth in its guides and as the pages are cut the blade is moved further in by

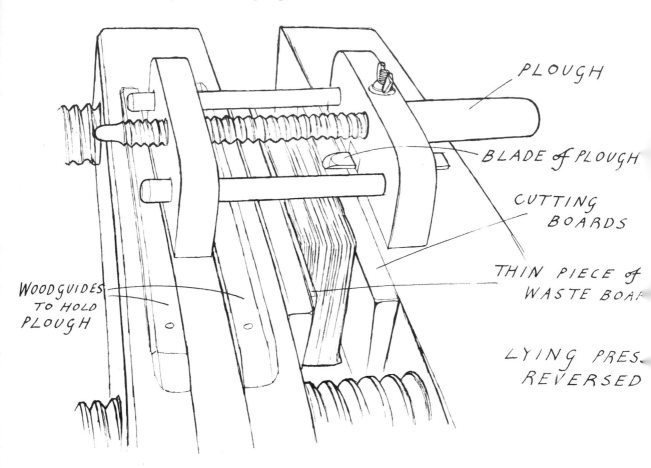

PLOUGH

BLADE of PLOUGH

CUTTING
BOARDS

THIN PIECE of
WASTE BOAR

WOOD GUIDES
TO HOLD
PLOUGH

LYING PRES.
REVERSED

means of the screw adjustment on the plough. This continues until one side of the book is trimmed, to be followed by the two other sides. Do not attempt this job on any important book until you have practised on one or two of no consequence.

6 Rebinding a cloth book

In this chapter you are ready to tackle your first rebinding of a book, in this case a cloth book.

You will need some material to cover the book itself – cloth, buckram, canvas etc. These may be obtained by the yard from various suppliers, but rather than confuse you with a description of all the different kinds of materials, I will nominate one, buckram, which I think serves most purposes for cloth rebinding. If you wish for details of the other materials it is possible to get patterns, showing colours etc. Buckram is very useful indeed. It is pleasant to look at, very strong, and comes in a good range of colours and usually two weights, single and double warp. The single is the lighter material, and will do for all except the very heavy books. Buckram is a smooth material and although not waterproof it stands up well to washing if a book becomes badly marked.

Mull is needed for the spine of the book and you will need some material for the boards of the book; in this case strawboard is used. It is also essential to have a lying press for this job, in order to put the round and grooves in the spine of the book.

So if you take your book that was sewn, endpapered, glued and possibly trimmed, you can now prepare it for its new boards.

Backing

It is a process we call backing and will necessitate the use of backing boards (fig. 49). These are similar to cutting boards, except that they slope away at the top instead of being flat. You will see that like the cutting boards they are wedge-shaped. This is to enable the book to be put into the press and tightened quickly by pushing down. The shape of the backing boards, being thinner at the bottom, enables this to happen. When the book with its backing boards either side is pushed into the press it gradually becomes locked as you push down. Another tool needed for this job is a backing hammer, which is used to shape the back of the book into its rounded state.

Before placing the book in the press to round the back, you need to get the spine into a rounded shape ready for hammering.

To do this take half of the pages of the book in your left hand with the fore edge of the book facing you. Then spread the pages at

77

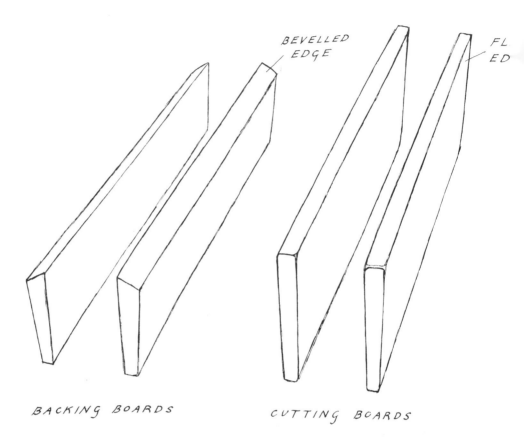

BEVELLED
EDGE

FL
ED

BACKING BOARDS

CUTTING BOARDS

the top so that they are nearer you than the middle ones. This will put a slight round in the spine. Using the backing hammer, give the spine several very sharp blows which should keep it in the correct shape. The book is then turned over and the operation repeated, but make sure that your rounding is equal on both sides.

To take the procedure from the start you should first take the book and lightly mark the endpaper with a line showing how much groove is required. As the strawboard will sit in this groove the measurement may be taken from that. There are various thicknesses of board but it will be fairly obvious which type is required for any specific book; you could refer to another volume which has already been bound if in any doubt. A pair of dividers is useful for marking such measurements but a rule will do. The pencil mark is made along the endpaper next to the spine (fig. 50) and a backing board is placed on that line. When both sides have their marks and backing boards correctly placed you can slip it in the press. Try and guess the approximate gap that the press should have before you try to insert the book, as it is so much easier than trying to do it with one hand while holding the book and boards with the other. You must not have the gap too wide or too narrow, but better a bit narrow than too wide as at least you will be able to insert part of the book.

When the book and boards are in the press only $\frac{1}{2}''$ of the backing board should be showing, to allow the press a good grip. This is essential because it is necessary to hammer the book quite hard. You will find it tricky to get the book into the correct position with both boards level on their lines – one board always

50 Putting backing boards to the book

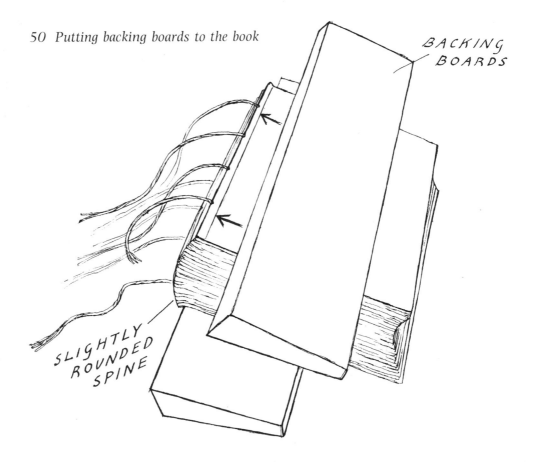

BACKING
BOARDS

SLIGHTLY
ROUNDED
SPINE

seems to move out of place — but with a little jiggling you should be able to manage it. By this I mean that once the book is in the press if a board is out of line you must try to work it back into place without taking the book out of the press. This will be made easier if the press is kept at just the right grip, not too loose, but not so hard that a great effort is needed to move anything. When you are satisfied that the book and boards are correctly placed you must tighten the press with the pin. It is necessary to have the book well gripped so do not be afraid to use force. A small point to watch for is that both ends of the press have the same gap. It is all too easy to tighten one screw more than the other so that the press is not gripping evenly.

You are now ready to put the round into your book. Taking the backing hammer position yourself so that you are looking down the length of the book and press. The first part of the process is most important, so make sure you get it right. The sections of the book must be persuaded to bend half one way and half the other (fig. 51). This starts from the very centre of the spine and can be

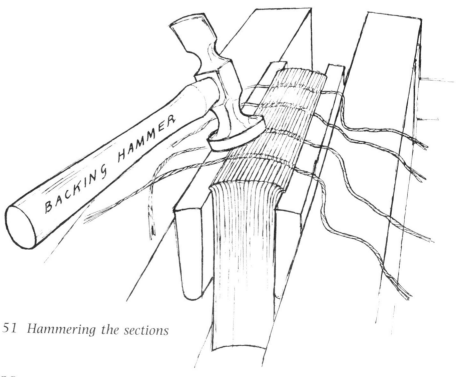

51 *Hammering the sections*

done by gently but firmly hammering the sections with a sideways motion. This is to say that the sections to the right of the middle are bent to the right, and likewise the other half to the left. If the sections are not bent correctly from the start they will tend to kink inside the book leaving unpleasant and damaging marks and making the book difficult to open and read. As the sections are hammered down you will notice that the gap you left above the backing boards is being flattened as the pressure from the other sections is brought to bear. You should finish up with the outer section lying flat on the backing board. This is best achieved by using the other side of the hammer, which is ideal for this job (fig. 52). It is easier to stand at the side of the press and just tap the edge down. Finally make sure that the overall rounding is smooth and even, using the hammer to tap down any unevenness. You should finish up with a neat 180° round as can be seen in figure 53. The book may now be taken out of the press and is ready to have the strawboard cut for the sides. If you have a board chopper this will be an easy job, otherwise you must cut by hand which

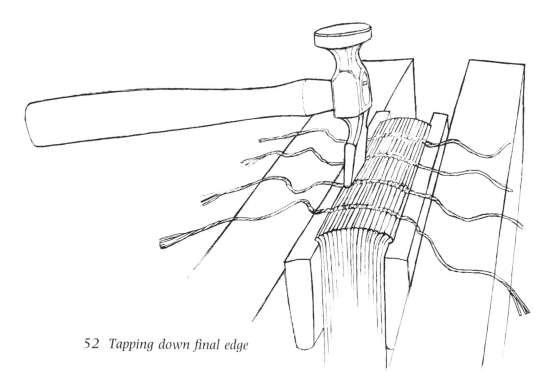

52 *Tapping down final edge*

53 The rounding of the book

CORRECT

TOO SPLIT
IN THE MIDDLE

NOT ENOUGH
ROUND ON
ONE SIDE

SECTIONS
SQUASHED
DOWN ON
ONE SIDE

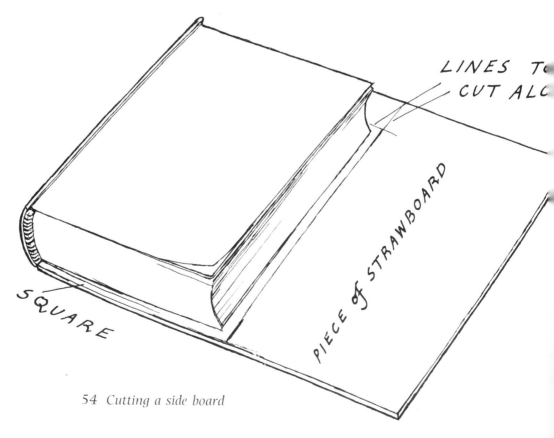

LINES T
CUT ALC

PIECE of STRAWBOARD

SQUARE

54 Cutting a side board

although laborious is still effective. Place the book on a clean piece of strawboard with the groove nestling tight to one edge (fig. 54). If the board and book are square with each other it should be possible to get your first edge without cutting (see previous diagram). Mark a similar square along the other two edges and join up the mark with a rule. Then cut along the lines you have marked and you have your board. It is as well to mark the board in one corner with a letter, say 'A', and also the book on the endpaper, so that you know that piece of board belongs to that side of the book. It is frustrating to get them mixed up after cutting, especially if you are cutting several at the same time.

Back Strip

When you have both boards cut and have ensured that they are the same size, you are ready to cut your back strip or hollow. Place the book in its boards and put into a small hand press. The back strip for most books can be taken from manilla which is a thickish paper. If the book is large a very thin strawboard is more suitable. You must be most careful to see that the grain of the manilla runs up and down the spine, otherwise it will not bend into a nice round, but crack and in time crack the cloth it is stuck to. To make sure you have the grain the right way, take the sheet of manilla and bend it till it is almost flat (fig. 55). If the grain is wrong (i.e. going across) the material will start to crack quite early and the resistance will be strong. When bending with the grain you should be able to get the manilla almost flat before it starts to crack. It soon becomes obvious once you have done it a few times, but I must stress that if you get this wrong your book will show your mistake quite clearly when the job is finished.

To cut the back strip, place the manilla on the spine of the book and bend it over the rounded back. The idea is to cut a strip of manilla which is a little wider than the spine but the same length as the boards. So, leaving a small overlap on the left of the back, mark a similar one on the other side (fig. 56). Check after marking that the top and bottom of the spine is the same width, as it is not uncommon for the width to vary a little. If it does vary you will have to allow for this when you cut the manilla strip, but if the

83

55 Folding back strip

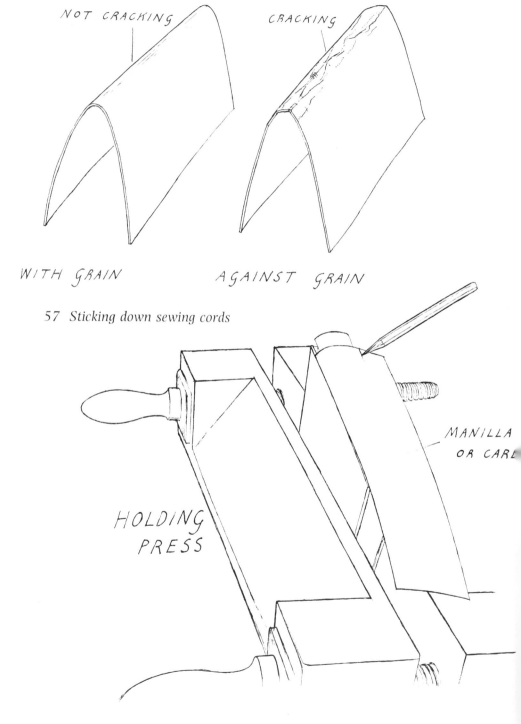

NOT CRACKING

CRACKING

WITH GRAIN

AGAINST GRAIN

57 Sticking down sewing cords

MANILLA
OR CARD

HOLDING
PRESS

previous instructions for binding have been carried out properly you should have an even rounded spine. Before starting on the covering material you should stick your sewing cords down. These should be cut to approximately 2″, separated and fluffed. The strings are made up of several strands and when separated may be fluffed up with the blunt side of a knife or palette knife, to make them soft so that when they are stuck down they will lie snugly on the endpaper. You may use paste or P.V.A. glue to do this, but not too much, just enough to make them stick down, and please keep them straight and neat (see fig. 57).

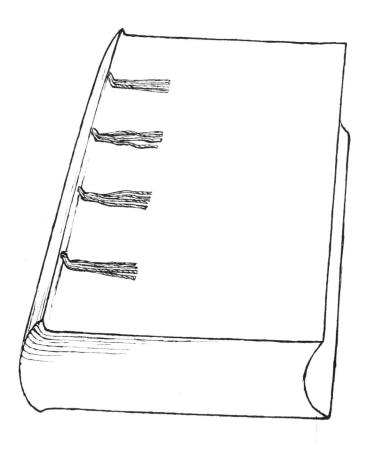

56 *Cutting a hollow for spine*

Mull

You will now need a piece of mull or linen for the strengthening of the endpapers. This can be glued on the spine leaving a small gap of $\frac{1}{2}''$ at top and bottom, and should be wide enough to cover the strings you have stuck down on the sides of the book. Cut your piece of mull exactly the right shape before gluing, then all you will have to do is place it on the spine and rub it firmly down into the glue. Mull is better than linen as it has holes in it to allow the glue to grip it really firmly. Once having fixed the mull, glue lightly again on the spine and cover with a piece of ordinary brown wrapping paper, watching that the grain again goes up and down the spine. The paper should cover the complete spine and may be cut off by folding the paper back and slitting down the fold as one would open a letter. This leaves the spine neat, tidy and, more important, strongly sealed. Do try to use thinnish glue – by this I mean not heavy treacly stuff, but not too watery either. The point is that too much glue makes the spine stiff and will eventually damage the pages. You should now have a book with its boards, back strip and mull which is ready for the outer covering, in this case buckram.

Buckram covering

When cutting the piece you need from a roll of buckram, place the book with fore-edge facing you, so that on cutting the buckram the longer length will cut into the roll (fig. 58). The tendency then is for the natural curve of the rolled buckram to wrap round the book. Allow a reasonable turn in, at the same time trying to keep the piece you are cutting as neat as possible so that later, when turning in, there will be less wastage. Having cut your buckram remember the inside of the roll is the outside of the book so don't glue the good side. This may sound elementary but I have seen professionals make this mistake quite often, when hurrying. You should roll the buckram into a cylinder the opposite way to its usual roll and this should enable it to sit flat on the paper you are using. Please make sure your glue is of a runny consistency. This is not an easy job at the best of times, but a heavy glue makes it impossible. It is possible to use P.V.A. glue which is, of course, cold, but do

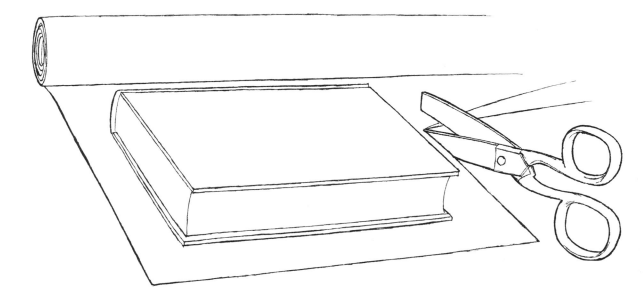

58 *Cutting out cloth for cover*

make the effort to use the real stuff if you can. The process using
P.V.A. is exactly the same.

Make sure you have everything to hand before starting this
operation as once started you do not want to have to search for
anything. We have a saying in the trade: 'The glue works faster
than you.' Obviously, if you mess around on this job your glue will
dry before you have finished, causing much gloom and
despondency. I am afraid the glue *will* work faster than you to start
with, but be assured that it is easy once you have developed
confidence. Again, I stress, keep your glue nice and thin and use a
good brush with long bristles; this will help greatly.

You should have: (1) large shears (2) folder (3) a pair of clean
pressing boards larger than the book to nip the book in (4) your
book with boards, back strip etc. (5) a large piece of waste paper on
which to glue.

Take the glue brush from its pot and wipe off the excess, leaving
enough to cover the buckram. Placing the left hand (if you are
right handed) firmly on the left hand side of the buckram, glue all
the right and middle of the sheet (fig. 59). You wish to keep the
glue even, so a nice splodging motion rather than a sliding one will

do the trick. If you slide the brush the glue tends to form lines which may show through the buckram on pressing, also the splodges seem to take longer to dry so try to get this effect.

When you have covered all the available area you will have to move your left hand so as to get at the unglued part. You will still have to hold the sheet so put two or three fingers on the glued bit to keep it steady. When you remove these fingers be careful not to move the sheet as it will be liable to adhere to your finger tips. Just a quick touch of the brush to those spots your fingers covered and you are ready to put the book on the sheet. The boards should be square with each other on the book and this is best done by tapping the book with boards, on a flat surface, on its tail, which means that the pages and boards are all level on the tail. The

59 *Gluing cloth for cover*

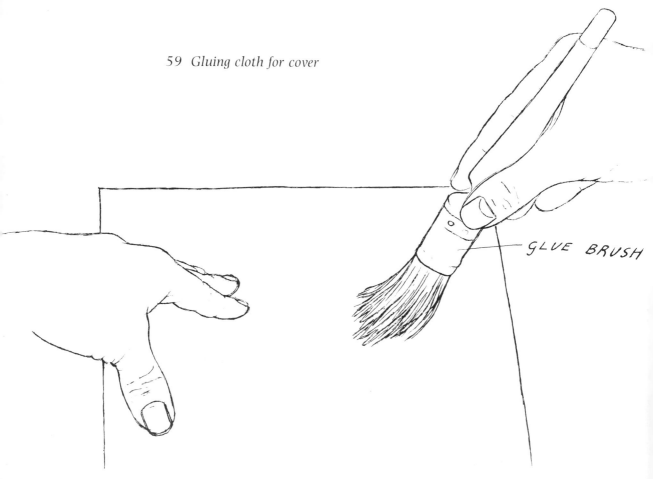

GLUE BRUSH

boards must, of course, be in their grooves next to the spine.

Place the book on the glued sheet with the spine facing inwards (fig. 60), allowing enough square for turn in (at least 1″). Make sure that the sheet and book are square with each other, otherwise you will not cover the second board properly. If you have cut the sheet as I suggested there will be no problem in doing the above.

Having placed the book square on the sheet take the back strip and insert it along the line of the first board, being careful to keep it straight. You may then pull the remaining buckram over the top of the other board, pulling it firmly tight and rubbing with the flat of the hand to ensure a temporary grip. On opening the new buckram and board case, lightly mark the book and one board on the inside with a line, using the folder; this will show which way the book goes back. Then if the back strip is not centralised take it out and replace it so that it is. If you have not been too slow this should be no problem.

Now cut the corners one by one leaving the thickness of the board for turning in, and using your folder turn in the sides or longer edges first (fig. 61), making very sure there are no gaps or 'pencil cases'. When you turn the ends in bend in the overlap at the corner, using your thumb nail (fig. 62).

61 Turning in cloth edges

62 Bending in corner overlap

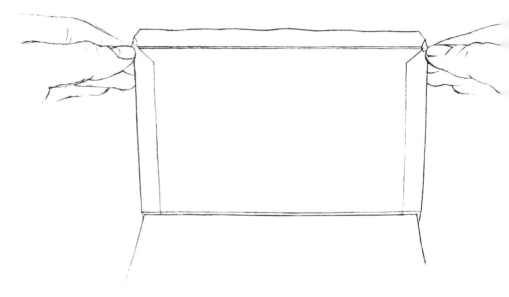

If you have cut the turn in too narrow you will not have enough
to cover the board, and should you have left too much you will
have an embarrassment of cloth which will be bulky. Having
turned in all the sides, turn the case over and rub the back strip to
ensure a good contact as this will, of course, not be pressed. Then
put the book back in the case and using the tip of the folder make
the ends of the back strip fit the contours of the round of the spine
(fig. 33). Placing the book and case between the clean pressing
boards put into the nipping press and wring down sharply for a
short time, i.e. 15 seconds.

90

Endpapers

Take the book out and check that everything is in order, not forgetting to look inside to see if the endpapers have stuck to odd bits of glue. If the paper has stuck to the buckram ease it off gently with the flat of a knife – otherwise you may damage the paper and have to renew it.

The case will have to be left for an hour or so before the endpapers may be pasted down. When this time has elapsed the process is as follows. You will need some cold water paste and the pressing boards that you used to nip the case in before. Make sure the book is in the correct position in its case i.e. the squares should be the same all the way round. Then lay the book down with the spine towards you and open the case, exposing the endpaper to be pasted (fig. 63). You may then begin pasting the endpaper,

63 *Pasting down endpaper*

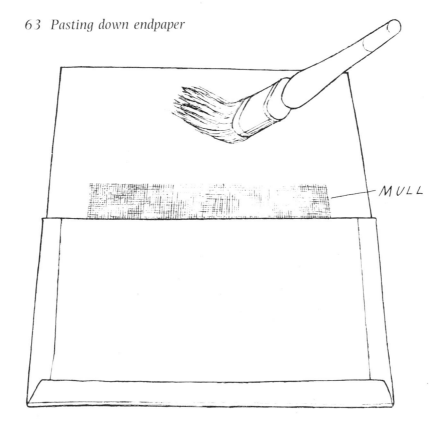

MULL

91

ensuring that you paste both sides of the mull flap. Try to get an even coat of paste, but not too thick, otherwise it will squeeze out when put in the press. When you have covered all the area to be pasted close the case again and turn the book over; you may now paste the other endpaper in the same way. Finally, shutting the case, place the pressing boards on either side of the book and put the whole lot into the nipping press, making sure that it is central in the press. Nip the book firmly and leave to set for a few hours, after which your book is finished except for any lettering you might want.

Just a quick word about the type of material you might use for this job. I have suggested buckram, but there are a number of other materials both heavier and lighter. The lighter cloths need careful treatment as too much paste or glue can easily soak through the material especially when nipping, so if you purchase a thin cloth be careful. With an art vellum or sundour for example you may have a lot of frustration and waste valuable material. A single or double warp buckram is by far the best material for most cloth bindings and is visually satisfying.

7 Rebinding quarter and half leather books

Now that you have re-bound a cloth book the next step is to re-bind in leather. There are several choices for the latter; quarter, half or full – quarter leather is just a leather spine, half is with corners added, and full is self-explanatory (see fig. 1). There is also a choice of materials e.g. morocco, niger, calf, sheep, cowhide. The two I shall describe are niger and calf as these two leathers will satisfy the wishes of 99% of people. The niger is a goat skin of good durability and is ideal for books from the nineteenth century onwards; eighteenth-century books and earlier are more likely to be bound in calf, although there are exceptions here and there. The niger leather is a very decorative material which has a quite pronounced grain, but this may be smoothed down by polishing and pressing to give a smooth surfaced book, which is very attractive and easy to tool in gold. When purchasing skins of niger care should be taken to buy decent quality leather that is not too heavy in thickness or in grain. In fact, I usually have my niger thinned by the tanners to make it softer and more malleable; also it means less work when you have to pare the top and bottom. Most leathers come in various colours: red, blue, green, black etc. and again niger seems natural when it is stained, whereas calf when coloured never seems quite right. Calf is, of course, a much thinner leather, but it has a beauty all its own especially when stained and polished to a tan colour with perhaps a few small black spots. The majority of older books were bound in calf or cowhide and although it wears well it is not as strong as niger. There is no reason why you may not bind any book in niger but it is better in my opinion to keep to the type of material and style that the book had originally.

The materials you will need for leather re-binding are calf and niger leather, some paste and mill board. This board is much stronger and more dense than strawboard and is a must for re-binding in leather. Strawboard would go soggy from the paste when the leather is attached, so you really must have some mill board. It is usually grey in colour, but I have seen and used black in heavy weights. I am afraid you will find it difficult to cut without a board chopper, but it can be done with an ordinary paring knife if one is persistent.

Boards and Strings

The boards may be cut in the same way as for the cloth book, but when cut they should be lined with thin paper on the inside, this being pasted on, and then given a quick nip in the press. Any wrapping paper will do for this job just as long as it is not too thick. The reasons for this will be made plain later.

You now have your book in its boards and you have put some round in the spine and grooves where the boards will sit, as described in the last chapter. If your book has been re-sewn you will need to lace the strings into the boards, this being a slightly different way of treating the strings to that for a cloth binding. The boards must be placed square in the book and the strings pulled so as to lie across the book (fig. 64). Mark with a biro where the strings go and make a notch for each one to sit in.

The idea is to attach the strings to the boards, but they must not show through the leather; therefore, they must be carefully set in. Two holes must be made for each string, one in the top and one from the bottom. The holes should be quite close but not so close as to run into each other (fig. 65). The holes can be made with a bradawl or any suitable pointed tool. Do not make your holes too small nor too big as they must be closed up again to leave no trace.

When you have made all your holes and notches, cut and paste the strings lightly and thread through the first hole inwards, quickly followed by the outward hole. You should finish up with all the ends of the strings showing on top and pulled tight with the board snuggled firmly in its groove. Put a waste piece of manilla between the board and the endpaper for protection then press down the holes to trap the strings very firmly. Cut off the excess pretty close to the board and taking a backing hammer and a knocking down iron, hammer the holes and strings flat and smooth (fig. 66). Lace in each board in turn, whereupon you will be ready to attach your three fold hollow and false bands if you require them.

Just before starting your hollow you should cut off the pointed parts of the corners of the boards next to the spine. This will enable the headcap of the leather to sit correctly (fig. 67).

64 *Preparing to lace in a board*

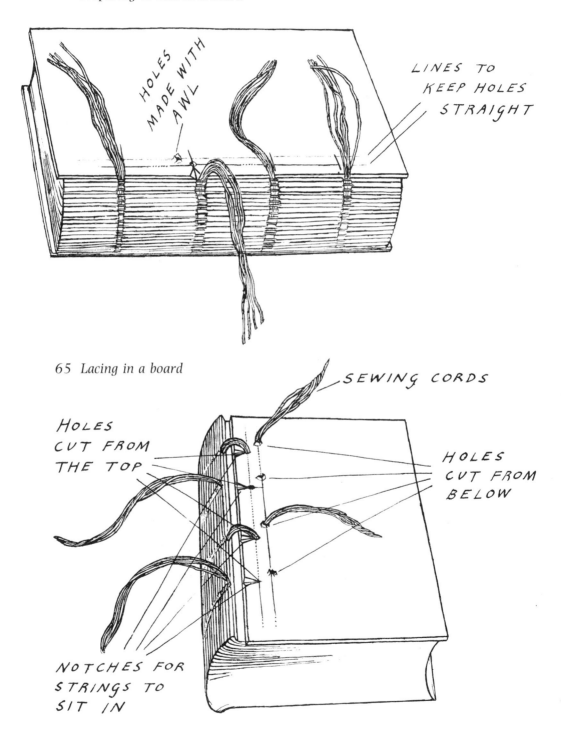

65 *Lacing in a board*

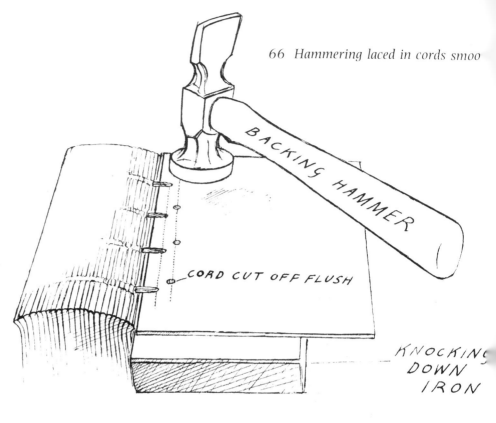

66 *Hammering laced in cords smoo*

BACKING HAMMER

CORD CUT OFF FLUSH

KNOCKING DOWN IRON

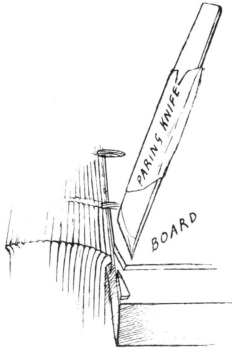

PARING KNIFE

BOARD

67 *Notching corner of board*

Cutting the leather

The leather can be cut when all the previous work has been completed and I shall be describing a half leather binding so if you require a quarter just eliminate the corners. You may cut your size of leather how you wish depending on how generous you wish to be with the leather, but on the head and tail allow enough to make a good turn in, i.e. on a 12″ book 1½″ turn in for each end. This will allow a little for any mistakes in paring which happen all too often to beginners. Corners are cut into triangles leaving a little less to turn in. Now comes the paring which I have explained earlier, but may I say again, take your time and get it right because if you cut holes in your leather it is spoilt, so go slowly and finish off with rough glass paper to get a nice even finish, making sure that the leather really is thin enough to turn in properly.

Sticking the leather

When paring is finished you will need the paste to stick the leather to the spine and boards. Cover the spine with a thin layer of paste and put to one side. Wet the leather to go on the spine with wet cotton wool, then paste well on the inside. Lay the leather on the spine and try to get it equal so that you have the same turn in top and tail and also on the sides. Taking both hands, press the leather firmly down onto the spine, sliding the even leather over the boards (fig. 34). Using the folder, press the leather down all along the boards and spine till you are satisfied that it is tight and smooth everywhere. Be careful to see that the boards stay in the right positions as they have a habit of moving while the leather is being applied, so keep a constant watch for this. Once the leather has been smoothed all over the back and sides you are ready to turn in the top and tail. Holding the book in the middle of the fore-edge let the boards drop away so that they lie flat on either side. It is easiest to work if you have the end you are turning in facing you on the edge of the work surface, then you may pull down the flap of the three fold hollow where the turning will go (see fig. 8).

The leather must be turned in neatly and in one piece. Slip the centre piece into the middle of the hollow and the rest will stick onto the inside of the two boards. If you find the leather becoming

97

kinked pull it out and start again as this job is impossible to get right if the leather is rucked up. You must also have the correct length of turn in, because if you have an excess there will be nowhere for it to go, making it necessary to cut some off. As the cu piece will not be pared down this will cause a nasty lump on the spine, so take care to see your turn in is just right before pasting the leather.

After you have turned in both ends check that everything is tight and that the boards are square with the book, then place the book closed with its spine towards you and open the board. You will find that the leather needs pressing down along the join and it is most important that you nip the leather between the board and the book so that you finish up with a sandwich of board/leather/book at an almost precise 90°. As the endpaper is to be stuck onto this joint you should see that a very neat job is done here (see fig. 35). Both boards must be opened and pressed in this way and I always have a quick look at this part of the binding before I finally leave the book to dry.

Capping

The head and tail, although turned in, now need to be finished off by what is known as capping. The cap is a small piece of leather on the top of the headband which is flattened to protect and round off the ends.

First take a piece of button thread long enough to go round the length of the book twice, and make a loop in one end. The thread should be passed right round the spine of the book settling into the notches you made in the boards at the head and tail. The cotton can now be pulled tight by passing the loose end through the loop, running back round one end of the book and tucking under itself whereupon it should lock and stay tight (see fig. 11). The reason for this should now be obvious: the leather has been pulled into the notches and is ready to be finished off. Take a folder and using the pointed end shape the leather into a pleasant curved effect, then tap down the rest to lie flat against the headband. If you find you have not enough leather to cover the headband you must pull out a little of the turn in, using finger and thumb to do so. Your finished cap should look like the one shown in the diagram.

This is the last part of the job and all that should be done now is to check that everything is as it should be and wash lightly all over the leather with some damp cotton wool to make sure you have left no excess paste on the surface. Then leave to dry. I would recommend that you leave the book resting so that the air can get at all the leather i.e. rest the book on the edge of a bench with a weight on one side, and the spine sticking out over the edge.

Raised bands

I have just described how to attach leather to the spine of a book which is smooth and plain. However, if your book has raised bands you will need to allow a little extra leather for them; also that leather must be pushed up and into the bands, so that the leather hugs each band in turn and may be nipped tight against it with a tool called, appropriately, band nippers. It is not essential to have this tool, but one cannot perform the work well without it. You will find that there is too much leather on the boards due to the extra needed for the bands and this must be smoothed out carefully, making sure you do not take away the leather you have pushed up the bands. As the bands are nipped you will soon see if you have allowed enough leather because, if not, as you nip one band it will pull leather from the one next door. Ideally each band should nip up tight on its own and stay like that, but you may find that you have to nip them again once or twice, depending on how springy the leather is. You should also press out the panels between the bands, making sure the leather is stuck flat to the spine and this may best be done with a very flat instrument such as a metal rule or the blunt end of a paring knife.

Corners

When the leather you have attached to the spine has dried you will be ready to attach the corners and these will be put on in pairs. It is hopeless to try and put the corners on if the edges are not pared nice and thin, so don't wet them till you are satisfied that this is done.

Wet and paste two corners and put them roughly in place. Turn the board over and start turning in each one roughly just to get them to stick in place. Then, using a folder, press down the turn in marrying up the leather where it joins at the point of the corner (fig. 68). Here you will find your leather must be thin or you will not get it neat, or worse still it will not stick at all. When both corners are turned in go over each one, being very firm with the folder, making sure the leather is stuck flat to the board everywhere then wiping off with wet cotton wool. As the board now has to be closed you should have some greaseproof paper to protect the endpaper from the wet leather. I have found the paper from cereal packets ideal for the job.

The corners need to dry; you may then start the process of trimming out. Take a pair of dividers and using the notches next to the head and tail (fig. 69) mark out a line at both ends which will cut out all the rough edges of the leather. Do this both sides of the spine and join up the marks with a rule, making a neat line. Also make a parallel line $\frac{1}{10}$" away from the first line, this will be the line you will cut along leaving the first line as a guide for your side paper or cloth. When you are trimming along the line use your paring knife which I hope will be very sharp, and make the cut at 45° angle rather than a sharp 90° one. This will make the filling in easier when you come to it. The corners can be trimmed as with the spine, using the dividers. Find the smallest corner and set the dividers to the length from the point where the leather ends, leaving enough to make your double mark.

Fill in
When you have cut both corners and sides you will need some thin strawboard, thick manilla or card to fill in. Take care to cut your fill in to the exact size so that when the cloth or paper side is attached there will be no holes or bumps. The fill in may be stuck to the board with either boiled glue or cold P.V.A. glue, making sure that just a thin coating is applied to avoid any squeezing out on the leather when you rub the material down with your folder.

68 Turning in a leather corner

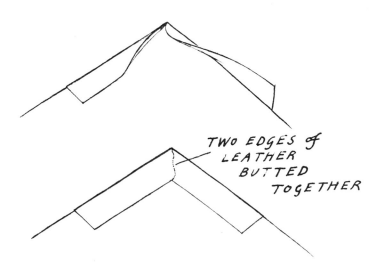

TWO EDGES of
LEATHER
BUTTED
TOGETHER

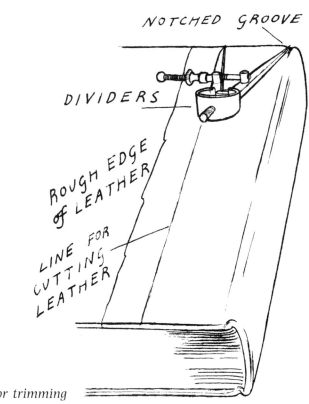

NOTCHED GROOVE

DIVIDERS

ROUGH EDGE
of LEATHER

LINE FOR
CUTTING
LEATHER

69 Marking leather spine for trimming

Side material

On completing the fill in for both sides you will need either a marbled paper or cloth to finish the outside of the book. If you choose a paper be sure the marbling matches each side and be careful to cut your longest edge very straight and square. This also applies to cloth; cut along the grain for the longest edge and laying the cloth or paper on the mark you made, bend the corners back to the similar lines you made on them, being careful to see that the material does not move from the first line, or obviously it will not fit all the lines when you stick it on. To ensure the latter has been correctly done put the material in position when you have cut it out and see that it is touching all the lines.

When you are ready to stick on the side material you may again use boiled glue or P.V.A. and again be careful to apply only the minimum amount. The easiest way to put the material on the book is to have the longest edge nearest you and concentrate on getting this exactly on the line, then check quickly to see that the corner lines are also right. You might have to slide up and down the line a bit to get your corners the same, but do make sure the long line is spot on; as nothing looks worse than a crooked side paper. Rub the paper down, using a piece of manilla so that the folder is not actually rubbing on your material, not forgetting to rub the edges of the boards and the turn in inside.

Endpapers

I usually like to trim out the surplus inside before the glue hardens too much so this is how it is done. Find a board or another book to put under the board you are trimming so that you do not break the joint of the book (fig. 70). Take the endpaper that will eventually be pasted down and put it in that position. You will now be able to judge quite easily how much of your turn in to keep. Using the dividers mark the required amount all round the three edges and trim off with your paring knife. This area will also have to be filled in using a piece of waste paper, white if possible. Before sticking down the endpaper it is helpful to ensure that it will cover the area you require, this being easily seen by folding the pasting down sheet into position to see how it will look. You must rub the

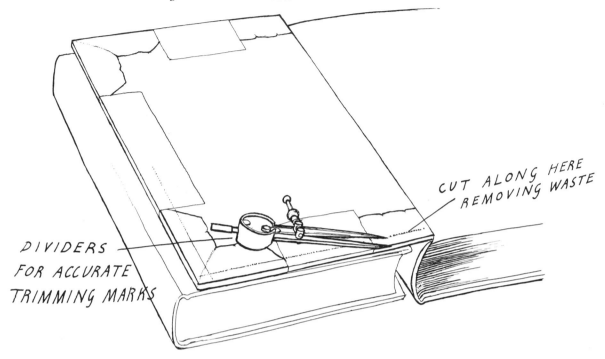

CUT ALONG HERE REMOVING WASTE

DIVIDERS FOR ACCURATE TRIMMING MARKS

joint a bit to get an exact fit because only by doing so can you see the amount of paper needed. If you find the paste down too long you can now cut off a piece and you are ready to apply your adhesive. As this is quite a tricky job it is as well to have everything organised, especially a CLEAN folder and working surface. I find that the P.V.A. glue is ideal for this job, much better than paste which can make the paper damp and soggy. A piece of waste paper is slipped in under the page you are pasting and then the whole area is given a thin coat including the joint (fig. 71).

I must stress again the importance of getting the amount of adhesive correct because it will squeeze out everywhere if you use too much. If you make sure the whole area is wet that will do fine.

Remove the waste paper and pull the pasted sheet onto the board it is to be stuck to, rubbing into the joint first. If you have measured and checked, as previously instructed, you will find it all goes down very easily. Then, taking the folder, rub all over the endpaper, paying extra attention to the joint, rubbing and checking to keep it tight. On no account must the book be closed once all

71 Pasting down endpaper of half-leather binding

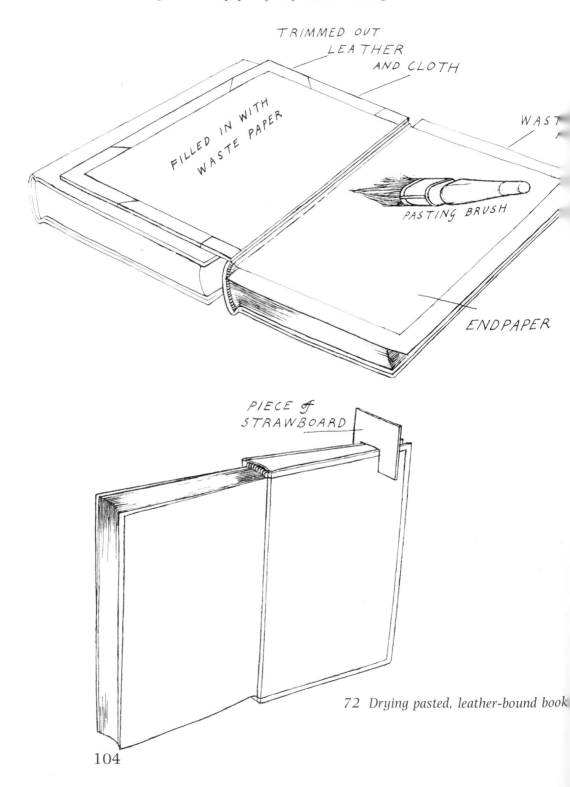

TRIMMED OUT
LEATHER
AND CLOTH

FILLED IN WITH
WASTE PAPER

WAST

PASTING BRUSH

ENDPAPER

PIECE of
STRAWBOARD

72 Drying pasted, leather-bound book

this is under way, as the joint or hinge, which you have carefully rubbed, will become unstuck. To do the other side you turn the whole over (hence the clean working surface) and then stick the other endpaper in the same way.

The book is now finished and must be left for the endpapers to dry, with the book standing as you can see in the diagram (fig. 72). A small piece of notched board will keep the two boards of the book back in the position you require. A couple of hours is all that is required for drying, then the book may be closed and checked to see that everything is as it should be. If you find that the endpapers are not stuck properly in the joints, it will be obvious that you did not rub them enough with your folder. Your only remedy then will be to tear out the endpaper and attach a new one – a great waste of time and material so do give your endpapers sufficient pressure when putting them down.

8 Rebinding full leather books

The ultimate in re-binding is to cover a volume in full leather whether it be in calf, morocco, niger or sheep. A full binding is the complete job and gives a pleasure all its own, especially, I find, when using the goat skins, morocco and niger. The latter may be polished and pressed when finished and really is most pleasing to the eye, even if one has bound thousands as I have. There is alway a pleasure in looking at the finished job.

The problems for the novice are considerable and full binding should not be attempted until good proficiency has been achieved with quarter and half binding. One reason for this is that materials are so expensive; to ruin a piece of leather big enough to fully cove the medium sized book would be most unfortunate, and could destroy one's confidence in starting another. The paring alone is much harder as a large area has to be thinned and one slip with th knife spells disaster. However, sooner or later the job of full binding should be tackled, so this is how it is done.

Cutting and Paring
I shall assume you have your book in its boards with the ties sewn in, hollow and maybe raised bands attached. I would advise, before you cut out your piece of leather, that a similar sized piece of waste paper be cut first. Lay the book on the paper and cut all round leaving $\frac{3}{4}''$ turn in.

You should now have an oblong piece of paper which can be tried in various places on your skin of leather to see where is the most suitable place to cut. Unless you require an immaculate piece of leather it will be obvious that one corner of the skin will waste the least leather. I have, on occasion, cut from the middle of a skin but only because money was no object and I wanted a perfect piece. If care is taken several medium sized books can be cut from one skin of leather and even then corners for half bindings can be made from the pieces left, at a later date. You cannot afford to waste materials these days. When you are cutting a piece of leather for a full binding try to keep it mathematically perfect as you will find that this will help you to pare the edges much more easily. When you start paring go all the way round the end of the piece thinning the first $\frac{1}{4}''$, then gradually working in from there. You may find it helpful to make a line with a biro or marker pen where the turn in starts, because your paring knife should not stray over this line. If you make any mark or hole on the wrong side of the line it will show up on the binding and nothing you can do will remove it.

However, it is not recommended to have an exact line where the paring begins so you should thin down the area around your line with glass paper and, in fact, this may be done to smooth out the whole of the pared turn in. You will have to take your time on this part of the job, as it is never easy. As previously mentioned the paring knife can be lethal, and just one stroke in a thousand can ruin your leather. This usually happens just as you say to yourself 'I will thin this bit a shade more and that will do'. Do not pare when you are tired, you need all your concentration, and stop for a rest frequently.

Pasting

When you have all the edges thinned correctly the leather can be attached to the book and as always only cold water paste should be used. The piece of leather is moistened with wet cotton wool and the paste applied. Do not forget to paste the hollow and bands (if any), also put just a little blob on each of the sewing cords to soften them. The pasted leather is then put on to the spine of the book making sure that an equal amount is left all round for the turn in.

Work from the spine and bands pushing the leather with the fingers hard down around the spine, as described in the previous chapter. Carefully smooth out any wrinkles at the sides of the boards, pushing excess leather to the edges very firmly and ensuring that the leather is hard to the board everywhere. If you have bands, nip them up at this stage and have a second go at the spine, to make sure all the leather is snug and tight. Check the SQUARES of the boards before proceeding any further and adjust if needed.

Turning in

The corners must be prepared for turning in and to do this the

leather for each one must be cut to the thickness of the board
(fig. 73). Do not cut these too close or the leather will not meet
when it is turned in; it is best to be a little generous, but if you hav
left too much the turn in will not be neat. When you have cut the
corners ready to be turned in you will find that the leather really
needs thinning again, so you will have to do this. Now the leather
wet from the paste and wet leather does not pare well, so take grea
care with the following instructions. Take a corner and using a
metal rule fold back the corner onto the rule exposing the
underside of the leather (fig. 74). Using the paring knife thin the
edge of the leather in one stroke; this is known as 'feathering'. You
need just to thin the piece that the shears cut as the rest of the
leather should already be thin enough. When you have treated all
four corners thus, start to turn in the longest sides, tucking in to th
hollow first. If you find the turn in has got a little dry by this time
spread some paste along with your finger. Turn in the two shorter
sides last and do not forget to put some greaseproof paper between
the wet leather and the book, especially the side you are not

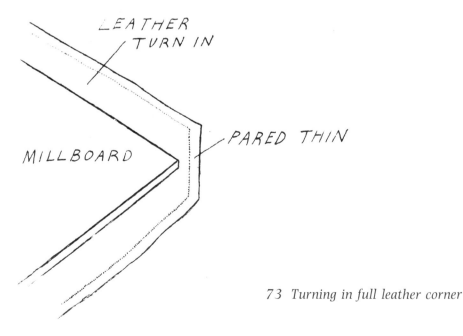

73 *Turning in full leather corner*

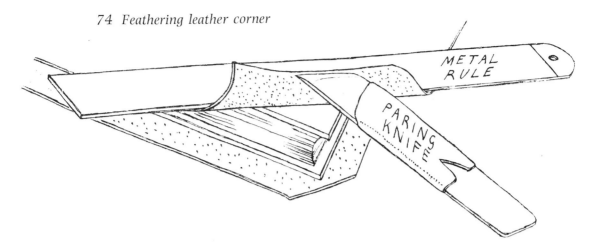

working on. It is very helpful to have a small piece of clean marble stone to rest on under the board on which you are working. Any suitable hard surface may be used, but be sure to use something. It is common to see a novice trying to complete the turn in by supporting the board with his free hand but this is stupid; both hands are needed to perform the job properly. Take trouble to get your turn in firmly stuck and especially the place where the leather joins at the corners. If you have pared and cut the leather properly this join will disappear as the two edges meet, but thick leather or clumsy cutting will prevent a neat job and if it will not stick it will be necessary to peel it back and pare some more off, very aggravating! When all the turn ins and corners are correct check the outside again, nipping up bands and head capping to finish.

Cleaning

It is most important to wash the leather with wet cotton wool as a very last job before putting the book to dry on a clean piece of white paper, with a piece of greaseproof underneath that. I have not repeated all the details of the previous chapter, many of which are needed for the above job, but I hope that these will be second nature to you before tackling full bindings.

Polishing and Plating

If you have been re-binding your books in niger or morocco you may like to have them polished and plated i.e. heavily flattened. This process is designed to please the eye and does not have any

75 *Polishing iron*

METAL

WOOD

great significance towards the protection of the book. The first stage of this treatment requires a polishing iron (fig. 75) which is heated up to quite a hot temperature by gas or electricity. To ensure the correct temperature put a drop of water on the reverse side of the iron, whereupon the water should just sizzle. This is to say that if it is too hot the water will sizzle in a much more agitated way and will form small balls which will quickly disappear instead of sizzling gently, spreading and then gradually disappearing. If you have the iron too hot you might easily blacken and burn the leather in one spot. When you think you have the iron at the right heat try it out on a small piece of spare leather first and even then do the back of the book before the front. Using the iron is mostly common sense, but one small tip may be helpful. That is, to let the top of the handle rest against the top of your shoulder as you polish (fig. 76) the sides of a book especially a full leather book. This will keep the iron steady, giving an even polish and also more pressure if the grain is a bit heavy.

When you are polishing the spine of a book it is only necessary to hold the iron in the hand working it firmly up and down.

The book may be plated if you desire, but it needs a lot of pressure to do this so a nipping press is required, also plating boards which are either very smooth metal plates or perspex sheets. A piece of thickish manilla is put in between the board and book at front and back, making sure the manilla is forced right into the joint of the endpaper. The book is then placed between the plating boards (make sure first that their surfaces are clean) and the whole lot put in the press and wrung down tightly to be left for at least 24 hours.

76 *Using a polishing iron*

77 *Some tools for gold lettering*

9 Gold finishing

In this chapter I shall give a very brief introduction to gold lettering and finishing. I must state from the outset that this part of book-binding really cannot be taught from books; it is far too complicated. The answer is to get tuition at a technical college where an expert will be able to show just how it is done. However, the principles are reasonably simple. Basically the leather or cloth is treated with a solution known as glair; the gold is laid on using gold leaf and a heated tool is pressed through the gold leaving an impression in the material.

Now, to go into that in a little more detail. The items you require are: (1) a stove for heating tools (2) sets of handle letters or fonts of type or both (3) gold leaf, which comes in books of tissue paper (4) pad of suede to lay the gold on for cutting (5) vaseline (6) cotton wool (7) petrol.

The pad of suede is most important and can be made quite easily by tacking a piece of reverse sheep or calf to a smooth flat piece of wood, which should have a little newspaper underneath to pad it out. The gold is removed from its tissue paper and placed on the pad using a clean table knife or similar. You cannot touch the gold as it will stick to your fingers. Also beware of draughts because the gold is so light that even a slight draught will move it. When you have it on the pad it must be covered when not in use. I use the top of a half dozen egg box for my cover. Your table knife should be just sharp enough to cut the gold, but not so sharp that it cuts into the suede, and it must be kept dry and clean at all times.

78 The finishing press and gold cushion

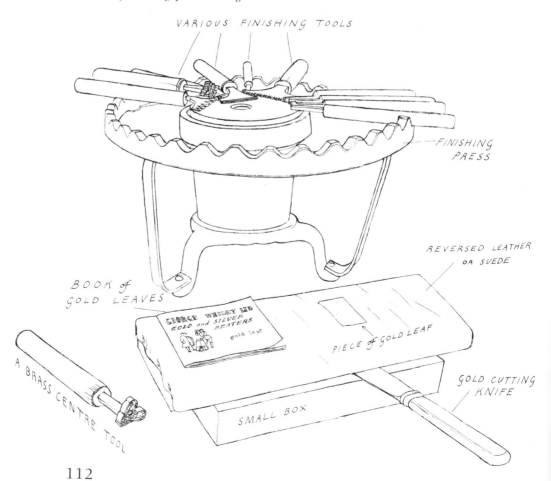

VARIOUS FINISHING TOOLS

FINISHING PRESS

REVERSED LEATHER OR SUEDE

BOOK OF GOLD LEAVES

GEORGE WHILEY LTD
GOLD and SILVER BEATERS
gold leaf

PIECE OF GOLD LEAF

A BRASS CENTRE TOOL

SMALL BOX

GOLD CUTTING KNIFE

The glair (I use bleached shellac glair) can be applied by brush or cotton wool. Normally two coats is enough, the first coat being allowed to dry before applying the second. Give the leather an hour to dry after applying the second coat. You may leave it for several days if you so desire; the gold will still stick after a long period of time. The gold is applied to the book over the whole area to be lettered or tooled. This means a lot is wasted, but this cannot be helped. The area to be tooled is smeared with a very thin application of vaseline which will hold the gold on the book so it can be worked. Cut the block of gold you require, then, taking a hand sized pad of cotton wool, make it slightly greasy by stroking it down the back of your hair; this will now pick up the gold from the suede and you can lay it on the book. The vaseline, being stickier than the cotton wool, will hold the gold and you can press it flat. You may have to put on more than one layer of gold, but as it is expensive try to make do with one layer. The gold now must be lined to guide where the letters will go and this is done using an ordinary piece of cotton which will cut easily through the gold, leaving a clear line (fig. 79). Mark the centre of the book, using dividers, and also if you are using handle letters, you can mark where each one will go, i.e.

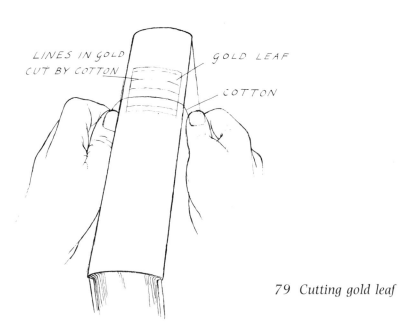

LINES IN GOLD
CUT BY COTTON

GOLD LEAF

COTTON

79 Cutting gold leaf

for a seven letter word, three marks either side of centre. If you want an exact guide mark out the letters on a piece of paper then you can place the paper on the book showing just where each letter goes. The letters should be set out on the stove to heat and the book is placed in a holding press with the spine tilted towards you and within easy reach. Check each tool for the correct heat as you did for the polishing iron. When the glair is a day or two old the tool may be used a little hotter than normal. Normal temperature would be just hot enough for the water to sizzle, perhaps slightly cooler than the polishing iron.

Each letter is then pressed into the gold in its appropriate place, taking care to keep the space between the letters the same. When all the lettering is completed the excess gold is rubbed off and the spine washed with a little petrol-soaked cotton wool and finally wiped dry with a soft clean cloth. Any surplus gold may be carefully removed with the points of dividers.

The process just described is a reasonably simple one, but it is very difficult to do well, and required hundreds of hours of practice, so by all means have a go on your own if you have the tools, but much frustration will be saved if you have a qualified instructor to help you.

Most large towns have a technical college, though not all have book-binding classes, but if there is a college near you with a class, I recommend you to give it a try, as the use of the tools and materials alone make it worthwhile. The tuition will vary of course, some instructors are better than others. There is a trend here and there to teach pupils gold finishing using gold foil, which I cannot recommend. This process is reasonable for the initialling of wallets, handbags, even the lettering of cloth books, but it will never do for finishing leather books and I would advise you to insist on gold leaf if it is available for leather work.

Finally, I hope this book will prove a help, enabling you to preserve and re-bind your own books. Practising this craft will give you endless pleasure and satisfaction not to mention saving you a deal of money, but do not forget that you will always be learning, no matter how many good jobs you complete.

Glossary

An explanation of book-binding terms including tools, equipment and materials.

ADHESIVES	Glues hot (animal) and cold (polyvinyl acetate emulsion, P.V.A.)
ARMING PRESS	Used for stamping heraldic arms on the cover of a book
ART CANVAS	A very heavy cloth
AWL	A pointed piece of metal in a rounded handle used for making holes in boards for the cords to be laced in
BACKING	The rounding and grooving of the spine of a book
BACK BOARDS	Two pieces of wood used in the above process
BACK SWELL	Unwanted air etc. in the spine of a book contracted
BACK SAW	Tenon saw
BAND NIPPERS	Tool used for pinching the leather up to a raised band on the spine of a book
BASIL	Rolled sheepskin
BLIND TOOLING	An impression made by a brass tool on damp leather
BLOCKING	Gold finishing using a machine
BOARD CUTTER	Hand guillotine for cutting the side boards for books
BOOK CLOTHS	General term for all cloth covering material
BOOK PLATE	A label, often with heraldic arms on it, pasted on to the inside of the front cover of a book
BRUSHES	Various round brushes used for pasting and gluing
BUCKRAM	A medium to heavy covering cloth
CALFSKIN	Leather from a calf
CALICO	A cheap linen
CAPPING	Forming the piece of material which covers the head band at the top and tail of the spine
CARTRIDGE PAPER	Machine made paper
CASED BOOK	A book which has had its cover made separately and then attached
COLLATION	Check to see if the pages of a book are complete and numbered correctly
CUSHION (GOLD)	Pad of suede for cutting gold leaf on
CUTTING BOARDS	Used in ploughing or cutting the edges of books
DECKLE EDGE	Uneven edge of hand made paper
DIVIDERS	Tool used for accurate space measuring
DRAWN IN BOARDS	The lacing of the boards to the sewing ties
FILLETS	A brass wheel for decorating a binding
FINISHING	Lettering and decoration to a completed binding
FOIL	Simulated gold or silver paper for lettering etc.
FOLDER	A bone tool
FORE EDGE	Front edge of a book, pronounced forrige as in porridge
FRENCH JOINT	A deep groove in the covering surface of a binding, parallel to and close to the spine
FULL BINDING	A complete covering of a book with one material
GLAIR	A liquid used to enable gold leaf to adhere to a binding
GLUE	See adhesive
GLUING UP	The sealing of the spine of a book with thin glue

115

GLUE POTS	Holding containers for hot glue
GOATSKIN	A grained leather from goats
GOLD LEAF	Paper-thin 24 carat gold used for finishing
GOLD TOOLING	The working of gold leaf into a binding
GRAIN DIRECTION	The easiest way a material bends
GUTTA-PERCHA	See single leaf bindings
GUARDS	A way of attaching a single leaf to a book
GUILLOTINE	Cutting machine for paper or board
HALF LEATHER	A book with leather spine and corners
HAMMER (BACKING)	Special hammer for rounding and backing a book
HEAD AND TAIL	Top and bottom of a book
HEADBANDS	A silk decoration at the top and tail of the spine
HEAD CAP	Material that covers and protects the headband
HEMP CORD	Sewing cord
HOLLOW BACK	Space between spine and the back of the binding
INSERT	Additional leaf added to a book
JOINTS	The inside of the hinge of the spine
KETTLE STITCH	A hitch knot when sewing a book
KNOCKING DOWN	
IRON	Used for taking the swelling out of a sewn book
LABEL	Lettering piece for spine or front of a book
LINSON	A cloth
LYING PRESS	Wooden press used for backing books etc.
MARBLE PAPER	Decorated paper
MILL BOARD	A strong, compact board for leather books
MOROCCO LEATHER	French cape goatskin
MULL	Coarse muslin
NIGER LEATHER	Nigerian goatskin
NIPPING PRESS	Press for compressing books
OILSTONES	For sharpening paring knives etc.
OVERSEWING	Joining several single pages together by sewing along one edge
PALETTE	Brass tool used for decorating the spine
PARCHMENT	Sheepskin vellum
PARING	The thinning of leather
PASTE	Adhesive made of flour and water
PASTE WASH	Method of washing cloth or leather with very watery paste
PENCIL CASE	A hollow caused by not pulling material tight to the edge of a board
PLOUGH	Used for cutting the edge of a book
POLISHING IRON	Iron for glossing and smoothing grained leather
POLYVINYL ACETATE EMULSION (P.V.A.)	A man made cold white glue which is dissolvent in water
PORTFOLIO	A case with flaps to hold a book or paper
PRESSING BOARDS	Boards for pressing or nipping a book in a press

PRESSING PLATES	As above but made of metal
PULLING	The disbanding of a book into sections
QUARTER LEATHER	Book bound with just a leather spine
REBACKING	The replacing of the spine
RECASING	The refixing of a loose book into its case
REXINE	A cloth
ROAN	Sheepskin
ROLL	A metal disc used in finishing with a continuous pattern
SEWING FRAME	Wooden frame for hand sewing books
SEWING KEYS	Pieces of metal used with a sewing frame
SHEARS	Large scissors
SHEEPSKIN	Leather from sheep
SIGNATURE	Letter or number on the bottom of the first page in each section of a book
SINGLE FOLD ENDPAPERS	Two leaves of paper attached to the book at the fold forming one continuous sheet when opened
SKIVER	Very thin leather used mainly for lettering labels
SLIP CASE	Case open at the spine end but enclosing the rest of the book
SOLANDER BOX	Dustproof box which completely encloses the book or papers it is protecting
SPINE	The back of a book
SPOKESHAVE	A tool sometimes used for paring leather
SPRINKLED EDGES	A method of spotting the edges of the pages of a book for decoration
SQUARE	The parts of the boards of a book which project to protect it from being damaged
STANDING PRESS	Large press for compressing a number of books at one time
STRAIGHT-EDGE	A metal rule
STRAW BOARD	Material used mainly for the boards of cloth books
SUNDOUR	A cloth
TIES	The extension of the sewing cords when the sewing is complete
TIGHT BACK	A book with the covering material stuck tight to the spine
TOOLING	The lettering or patterning of a binding with brass tools
TRIMMING OUT	Process of geometrically cutting out the rough parts of the leather etc. after it has been applied to a binding and dried
TYPE	Brass lettering
VELLUM	Stretched skin
WARPING	The bending of boards when drying out
WOODEN BOARDS	Very early books pre 1700 were often bound using solid wood for boards

List of materials and suppliers

ADHESIVES	Hewit, Monarch
BLOCKING BRASSES	Mackrell
BOARDS, MILL	Brown Brough, Spicer-Cowan
BOARDS, STRAW	Brown Brough, Spicer-Cowan, Red Gate
BOOK CLOTHS	Bentley Smith, Dryad, Hewit, Russell, Winterbottom
CORDS, HEMP	Hewit, Russell, Dryad
FINISHING STORES	Hewit, Russell, Dryad
FINISHING TOOLS	Mackrell, Whiley Winter
FOLDERS, BONE	Dryad, Hewit, Russell
FURBISHING CREAM	Arthur Rich & Partners (*Pliancreme*)
GOLD FOIL	American Roll Leaf, Red Gate
GOLD LEAF	Whiley
HEADBAND TAPE	Hewit, Russell
LEATHER TAPE	Hewit, Russell
MULL TAPE	Hewit, Russell, Red Gate
PAPER END ETC.	Hewit, Russell, Lawrence, Spicer-Cowan
PAPER, MARBLED	Cockerell, Rainbow patterns, Hewit
TAPE	Hewit, Dryad, Russell
THREAD, SEWING	Barbour Threads, Dryad, Hewit, Russell
TOOLS GENERAL	Dryad, Hewit, Russell
TYPE LETTERING	Mackrell, Hewit, Russell, Winter
TYPE HOLDERS	Mackrell, Hewit
VELLUM	Band, Hewit

For the amateur especially: Russell Bookcrafts, Hitchin, Herts; Dryad Handicrafts, Northgates, Leicester. I would also recommend J. Hewit and Sons with whom I have done business for many years. They are suppliers to the trade of course, but individuals may buy most book-binding materials (especially leather).

The following is a general list of suppliers in alphabetical order:
American Roll Leaf Co Ltd, 30, Canal Street, Manchester
Band, H. & Co, Brent Way, High Street, Brentford, Middx
Barbour Threads Ltd, Hilden House, Frogmore, London S.W.8
Bentley Smith & Co Ltd, Bengal Mill, Upper Hellena Street, Manchester 10
Brown, Brough & Co Ltd, 3 Dufferin St, London EC1Y 8SD
Cockerell, Douglas & Son, Riversdale, Grantchester, Cambridge
Compton Marbles, Compton Press, Compton, Chamberlayne near
    Salisbury, Wilts
Dryad Handicrafts, Northgates, Leicester
Hewit & Sons, 97 St John St, London E.C.1
Lawrence, T. N. & Son, 2 Bleeding Heart Yard, Greville St, London E.C.1
Monarch, Schoolfield Rd, West Thurrock, Essex

Mackrell, T. & Co, Industrial Estate West, Colchester Rd, Witham, Essex
Red Gate Converters (Bolton) Ltd, Red Bridge Mill, Ainsworth,
    Bolton BL2 5PD, Lancs
Rich, Arthur, Mount Pleasant, Belper, Derby
Russell Bookcrafts, Hitchin, Herts
Spicer-Cowan Ltd, 19 New Bridge St, London E.C.4
Thames Strawboard Co, Barrington House, Gresham St, London E.C.2
Whiley, Geo. M., Victoria Rd, Ruislip, Middx
Winter & Co Ltd, 12 Charterhouse Buildings, London E.C.1
Winterbottom Products, Victoria Mills, Weaste, Salford 8, Manchester

U.S.A. SUPPLIERS

Art Handcrafts Leather Company, 3512 Flatlands Avenue, Brooklyn,
    N.Y. 11234
Basic Crafts Company, 1201 Broadway, New York, N.Y. 10001
Broadhead-Garrett Co., 1233 Broadway, Sacramento, Calif. 95818
Gane Brothers and Lane, Inc., 1400 Greenleaf Avenue, Elk Grove Village,
    Ill. 60607; *with branches at* 4115 Forest Park Blvd., St. Louis, Mo.
    63108; 161 MacQuesten Pky. So., Mt. Vernon, N.Y. 10550; 1511
    Prudential Drive, Dallas, Texas 75235; 218 Littlefield Avenue, South
    San Francisco, Calif. 94080; 150 Mendel Drive, S.W., Atlanta, Ga.
    30336; 4697 East 48th Street, Vernon, Calif. 90058
A.I. Friedman, 25 West 45th Street, New York, N.Y. 10036
Paxton Equipment Supply, 7401 South Pulaski Road, Chicago, Ill. 60629
Ernest Schaefer, Inc., 731 Lehigh Avenue, Union City, N.J. 07083
Talas, Division of Technical Library Service, 104 Fifth Avenue, New York,
    N.Y. 10011
Henry Westphal and Co., Inc., 4 East 32nd Street, New York, N.Y. 10016

Index

Adhesives (see glue, paste)
Awls 10

Backing 77
Back strip 83
Band nippers 10, 99
Bands, raised 41, 99
Board cutter 75
Boards, backing 33, 78, 79
  book 82
  cutting 62, 76, 78
Brushes 32, 59
Buckram 86

Calfskin 14, 93
Cord (sewing) 63, 67
Corners, leather 24, 99
Cowhide 14

Disbinding 57
Dividers 10, 24, 101, 103

Edges, ploughing 74—76
Endpapers 31, 70, 91
Equipment (tools) 10

Finishing (gold) 111—113
Folder 10
Fore-edge 8
Full binding 106
Furbishing 27

Glair 112
Glue 32
Glue pot 32
Gluing up 73
Goat skin 14, 93
Gold leaf 112—113
Gold cushion 112
Gold tooling 111—113

Half leather 93
Hammers 10, 80, 81, 96
Heads and tails 17
Headbands 44—47
Head capping 23, 98
Hollow back 37

Kettle stitch 67
Knives 10
Knocking down iron 72

Lacing in 95
Lifting leather 16
Lying press 33

Millboard 93
Morocco leather 93
Mull 31, 86

Niger (Nigerian goat skin) 14, 93
Nipping press 59, 60

Oilstone 12

Paring (leather) 22
Paring knives 10
Pasting down 91, 104
Paste (flour) 13
Paste brushes 91, 104
Phillip's hollow 35
Polishing leather 110
Pressing 71, 72
Pulling 57
P.V.A. glue 86

Quarter leather 93

Rebacking cloth 29, 48
Rebacking leather 30, 53
Rebacking paper 52
Rebinding cloth 77
Rebinding $\frac{1}{4}$, $\frac{1}{2}$ leather 93
Rebinding full leather 106
Rounding 80, 82

Saw, tenon 10
Sawing 58, 62
Sewing 63
Sewing frame 63
Sewing thread 67
Sewing needles 66
Sewing keys 65
Shears 10
Sheepskin 14
Square of board 8
Staining leather 14
Strawboard 83

Tears, repairing of 26
Tooling (gold) 111—113
Trimming out 102
Type for lettering 111
Turning in 20, 50, 90